T0380225

WATEHICA

(that which you hold dear)

Poems and Stories by

Eya Mani

Order this book online at www.trafford.com
or email orders@trafford.com

Most Trafford titles are also available at major online book retailers.

Print information available on the last page.

ISBN: 978-1-5536-9772-5 (sc)
ISBN: 978-1-4122-4931-7 (e)

Trafford rev. 02/08/2021

 www.trafford.com

North America & international
toll-free: 844-688-6899 (USA & Canada)
fax: 812 355 4082

TABLE OF CONTENTS
(not necessarily in this order...)

FOREWORD

FOREWORD

Eya Mani is "Speaks Walking" in the Lakota language. My maternal grandfather was John Luke Speaks Walking for whom I have been named. Eya Mani came to the Standing Rock Reservation in the early 1900's from the Ft. Berthold Reservation North of Bismarck, ND.

Eya Mani married Lucy Tiger of the Wakpala Community and my mother was born in 1923......she is an only child. After Lucy's death in 1926, Eya Mani met and married a woman from the Rock Creek (Bullhead) Community named Josephine DeRockbraine, who raised and nurtured my mother until her death in 1945.

Eya Mani raised my mother alone...never remarrying. He moved north of the trading post in Rock Creek and bought 40 acres of land on which he planted corn, squash, potatoes, and assorted garden vegetables. Each year at harvest Eya Mani would invite the widows, the elderly, and those unable to raise crops, to come and take what they would need for the coming winter, and he would keep what was left.

Eya Mani, a WWI Veteran, was also a respected member of the council...working always for the People.

Eya Mani also had a reputation as a bootlegger, but what most didn't know, he took the profits from his bootlegging operation and returned it to the orphans, the fatherless, and the widows of the community. There was no welfare system in place on Standing Rock then and the people pretty much had to depend on each other yet to survive.

It is in keeping with this tradition of always helping the People, caring for those less fortunate, and also in keeping the promise, "to not let anyone forget", that these stories and writings are being completed...

WATEHICA is a collection of Poems and Short Stories...I know you will enjoy reading them as much as I have enjoyed sharing them...

Hau!

FOREWORD

"Kola Tokilalahe" is a song the Lakota sing in honor of their fallen veterans...and it means, "My friend, where have you gone...?"

I first heard this song when my uncle was missing...he was a veteran, and he was a very good person.

By that I mean he did for the People as in the old way...he was not an idle person, that was not his nature. He did what he could and when that was not enough, he went out and found things to do for the People.

As in "Soup and Frybread", my early upbringing had many of these kinds of persons and personalities I learned from daily, by observing and listening to what they had to say.

My grandparents had cattle and horses, and my father also had horses, so we had the opportunity to learn how to cowboy in the old way. Breaking horses as the old timers did and learning new ways although never having the desire to ride in competition in the rodeo's.

To me caring for the animals was as important as breaking them properly for riding and working cattle. I didn't want to be around when someone was abusing an animal, as I considered them to be doing at the rodeo.

In this collection of writings I wanted to share a time when the life experience was just that, a good experience...sometimes difficult but never overpowering.

Today's life experience somehow seems to end with someone, or everyone, going to counseling.

This seems self defeating, because today we have counselors who cannot maintain a relationship with their own wives and children...yet are allowed to minister to others.

Once one of my uncles said to me, "Know how to play this?" (as he picked up a guitar) "You know...when you feel bad you can sing and play a song that will make you feel better...or if you feel good you can sing and play a song that will help you remember the time..."

All my uncles were musicians and singers, as are my cousins.

Since I was a male child my uncles had more to teaching me than my aunts, but it was the aunts who did the nurturing and caring...and we were never treated as if we were not a member of their family.

Most of my uncles and aunts, and certainly all my grandparents have long since gone, and very few of my relatives remain who are older than my generation, and it is to them I dedicate this work, and I can remember, "Kola, Tokilalahe?"...

(do not answer that question)

Hau!

ACKNOWLEDGEMENTS

In June 1998 a man died and was buried in Fort Collins, Colorado. He was my friend, yet I did not attend his wake or his funeral. To this day I am still ashamed for not having attended. Being unable to attend physically, or financially does not seem to make any difference, my guilt is enormous. Because the gifts he has given me have completely opened up a new life and a new world for me.

You see, poverty is not just a word, poverty is a living breathing entity that can strip you of your humanity, poverty can embarrass you, and poverty can make you into the worst sort of person imaginable. (A seemingly thankless person!!!)

(Tradition dictates that someone from our family attend the funeral of such a well known and respected man, and so I sent my eldest son to represent the family.)

I first met this man in October 1990. I had been making miniature Tipi's with my friend Pat Loves War and my brother Joseph Earl. This man came in and looked around and asked if I made full sized Tipi's and said he would be back, then he was gone.

About one month later this man came back to my house and unloaded an industrial sewing machine and about 32 yds of material. I made a 12 ft. Tipi, Pat painted it, and together we made a trip to Ft. Collins to return the gift.

Through out the years we have kept tabs on each other and we have even visited each others homes from time to time. Our families have become more than friends and someday I know I will be able to properly return all the goodness, and kindness, and the generosity of this incredible human being.

With this, my first and finest effort, I wish to dedicate this small collection of Lakota works to him. He has retaught me the meaning of Love.....we can only love one another by caring and sharing.....

Louis Andrew Trujillo.....
        loving husband.....
                loving father.....
                        Marine....
                                and Warrior

Semper Fi

Hau!

ACKNOWLEDGEMENTS

MITAKUYE OYASIN
(To All My Relatives)

Growing up in the early 50's and 60's on the Standing Rock Indian Reservation in South Dakota I've had the opportunity to experience what is probably the very end of an era, an era where our people were still drug and alcohol free. Maybe not completely alcohol free but certainly there were no drugs available at that time for anyone's availability to abuse.

Because the Lakota people were a Warrior Society, it was natural for our young men to join the Armed Forces of the United States. One of the things our young men brought home was alcohol use and all its problems.

In my home community of Rock Creek (Bullhead, SD) there were only two people that had vehicles in them days. One was the storekeeper, Mr. Dempsey Harris and the other person was Mr. John Thompson, everyone else used teams of horses and wagons to get around.

Being raised by my Grandparents and Aunts and Uncles, we traveled from village to village by wagon, sometimes these trips took 2-3 days, depending on where it was we were going and who we were going to see. My Grandparents always carried a big square Army style tent in which we stayed during our visits. We always took our own food and water and sometimes spare horses which we kids sometimes rode around exploring while the Grandparents did their visiting.

These were very good times for us children and we had learning experiences that I often wish I could duplicate for my own children. When one of us boys did something that was not acceptable to the older folks, we were never corrected by physical punishment. My Grand mother would simply say, "Takoja, Lakota tuweni hecunsni", meaning "My grand child, the Lakota never do that, that is for the others to do!"

This would start a chain of events. First, depending on who did what?, one of the Aunts or the Uncles would take the offending party aside and they would do something together, something constructive and usually something that would benefit the family in its completion. This interactivity brought the relationships closer to one another and the learning experience that was shared was also life improving, so its benefits were both far reaching and instructional.....but one had to pay attention.

So to that end, I wish to acknowledge my many relatives, Grandparents, Uncles and Aunts, Cousins, Nieces and Nephews, I hope that by my writings they will understand that *although we are not allowed to teach many of the things that made our Society what it was...some of us still know and we will not allow them to be forgotten.*

Special consideration is given to my Aunts; Mrs. Ella Mae Kills Pretty Enemy, Mrs. Rachel Otter Robe, Mrs. Ada Red Horse, Mrs. Johanna Flyinghorse, and Mrs. Ethel Long Elk, and so many others I have no room here to name...without them I would have been lost...thank you.

I can never repay the kindness or the love that you have shown me, my brothers and our other relatives.

It is with very special and fond memories that I mention my paternal grandmother Mrs. Bertha Little Eagle Mutchler and my grandfather, Mr. Charles William Mutchler. I have learned so many things from being in your presence, I wish you had a chance to meet my children and grandchildren, they would have loved you as I have. You have taught me well and I will do my best to make you proud of me.

Thank you.

Hau!

THE LORD'S PRAYER
(Lakota Translation)

From the Author

It is customary to pray before any event of the people begins...whether it be a meeting, a gathering of The People, a Pow Wow, or singularly at the dawning of a new day.

Most Lakota prayers are said from the heart and are not written or recited from memory as the Lord's prayer is, however it is in observance of the Almighty and the gifts that he has provided the author of these writings, that this Lakota translation is included. Although the translation is written in the dialect of our brothers to the east, the Sisseton-Wahpeton, the author has taken the liberty of changing the pronounciation to be that of the Hunkpapa Band of Lakota of the Standing Rock Reservation.

It is in the Spirit of sharing that this translation is included...no offense is intended but if there is offense taken, it is with the humblest of apologies that I submit this work...

Hau!

(Eya Mani-1999)

ITANCAN TAWOCEKIYE KIN
(The Lord's Prayer...a Lakota translation)

Our father, who art in Heaven
(Ateunyanpi Mahpiya ekta nanke cin)

Hallowed be thy name
(Nicaje wakanlapi kte)

Thy kingdom come
(Nitokiconze u kte)

Thy will be done on earth
(Nitawacin maka akan econpi nunwe)

As it is in heaven
(Mahpiya ekta iyececa)

Give us this day our daily bread
(Anpetukinle anpetu woyute unqupo)

And forgive us our trespasses
(Qa waunhtanipi unkicicajuju miye)

As we forgive those who tresspass against us
(Tona sicaya ecaunkicoupi wicunkicicajujupi kin iyececa)

And lead us not into temptation
(Qa taku wawiyutan el unkayapi sni ye)

But deliver us from evil
(Tuka sica cin etanhan eunyaku po)

For thine is the kingdom
(Wokiconze kin he niye nitawa)

The power
(Qa wowasake kin)

and the Glory
(Qa wowitan kin)

For ever
(Owihanke wanica)

Amen
(Hau!! Mitakuye Oyasin!!)

"AND YOU TOUCHED ME"

From the Author

In 1998 a tragedy occurred in our family...one of our nephews was shot and killed in Minneapolis, Minnesota.

The killing had taken place right in front of his home...his mother had heard the gunshots and had run out to find her son lying dead in the street...apparently a gang had been after him repeatedly to 'join' their gang, when he refused, they had him killed.

A few days after Anthony's killing, the shooter was himself found in a trash dumpster, the reason for his killing is unknown.

Our family set up a Scholarship and a Memorial in Anthony's memory, to honor those students of Smee School in Wakpala who excelled in academics, sportsmanship, school attendance and citizenship. It is a four-year Scholarship and Memorial beginning with the Freshmen class, when Anthony would have been a Freshmen, ending when he would have been a Senior.

This poem was written on very short notice. It was read at the first year (1998-99) presentation of Awards on Graduation in May 1999.

Anthony's death came at a time when tragedy was touching a lot of families on Standing Rock Reservation. Our young people, mostly male, were killing themselves and our Tribal Government did not know what to do.

About this same time I had a radio talk show I called "Ideas-Hopes-and Dreams Inc." which I had named after a discussion group a few of my cousins, my brother and I created...We would sit for hours and discuss better ways and find solutions for the problems our Tribal Council seemed unable to cope with.

It is ironic that the Tribal Leadership's inability to handle seemingly basic human problems would spell the demise of my radio show. We were not allowed to discuss certain things on the radio...we were censored to death...and many good radio program hosts bit the dust during this time.

I cried uncontrollably as I ended this poem...remembering all those young lives lost in dispair and hopelessness...it is Lakota Culture to share...misfortune and fortune as well...because the actions of one do affect the many, nothing was hidden, but all was discussed and decisions were made by the Elders and the Leadership...but that all seems so very long ago...

Now I offer you..."AND YOU TOUCHED ME!"...for Anthony

Hau!

"AND YOU TOUCHED ME"

A Poem
by
Eya Mani

"What can I tell you?"
"my Dad?, my Grandmother?, my Nephew?"
"If you were here?"

"I've heard some of the young ones say,"
'It doesn't pay to be good!'..... 'I wish I was never born!'
'No one cares about the Youth!'

"From where you are, on the other side,"
"I know you could tell them differently."
"You could tell them someone does care..."

"And it does pay to be good...and that life is the greatest gift of all,"
"You could tell them that life is meant to be a challenge...daily"
"but there is help for those who want help?"
"and sometimes they might have to ask for help...more than once."

"You could tell them that although we can't give them what they want?"
"We will try to give them what they need?...even though it sometimes is not enough?"
"And you could tell them that 'we are all related' and they will never be alone...
although sometimes it feels like it?"

"You could tell them that they have touched our lives in so many ways...
that they probably have not realized it?"
"If they ask for an example?...You could tell them that your sister helped one
of her Uncles quit smoking...simply by asking him why he smoked?"

"and you could tell them that we will love them no matter what they do...
because the choice has been theirs alone to make?"
"and you could tell them that smiles are better than tears and angry words."

"But most of all you could tell them that they have made a difference in our lives...
everyday...with their kind 'Hello's....with their honest smiles when they wave to us...
and we don't want to be missing them...

like I am missing you now"

(for Anthony)
May 1999

Hau!

BLACKHORSE

From the Author

After the settling of the Reservations in the late 1800's the US Army authorized the Church's to enter the newly established territories and Reservations and "Educate" the inhabitants.

As Forts were established missionaries were encouraged to also come and help in the "assimilation" of these newly found heathen. Since many of the inhabitants lived in very rural areas, other means to achieve their ends had to be found to bring the word to the natives. Kidnapping was very common during this time and continued on into the 1900's and those kidnapped were sent away to Government Schools and Church Schools to be educated in the White Man's way of life.

Life in these "Boarding Schools" was a nightmare for these young Lakota children, their hair was cut, they were beaten, they were forbidden to speak their Native tongue, and they were humiliated in every manner imaginable, including "Sexual Rape" and continued "Sexual Molestation" by the Priests and the Nuns.

My Grandmother was one victim...

In many cases the kidnapped were kept away from their home for very long periods of time, as was my Grandmother. She was taken at 4 yrs and ran away and returned home when she was 13. To avoid being returned to the Boarding School system she got married and started a family.

Shortly before her death in 1987 my Grandmother came to our home and made her wishes known. She was going away to die and she wanted her clothing burned. But more than that, she wanted my family to stay at the family homestead and welcome all those who came to visit, just as she and my Grandfather had done during their time together... and she made me promise that I would not let anyone forget.

Although we were forced to leave the family homestead in 1989, in keeping with her other wish I am trying to tell the stories as they had occurred.

Black Horse is her story...and my father's as well.

Hau!

BLACK HORSE

A Poem
by
Eya Mani

They came when no one was watching

they came in the name of the Lord

They took them when no one could stop them

they took them in the name of the Lord

No one bothered to tell her parents

they came in the name of the Lord

Her and twenty of her playmates

They took in the name of the Lord

They took her to St. Elizabeth

To be raised in the name of the Lord

They gave her the Christian name Bertha

and they raised her in the name of the Lord

They called her names and they beat her

...beat her in the name of the Lord

They cut her hair and they changed her dress

and she prayed in the name of the Lord

From Standing Rock to Sisseton

she was taken in the name of the Lord

and from Sisseton to Phoenix

all was done...done in the name of the Lord

She was only four years old when she was taken

Taken in the name of the Lord

Now she was thirteen and fully schooled

Schooled in the name of the Lord

She was married and they had a son

All in the name of the Lord

But she taught him in the old way and

Not in the way of the Lord

He was only four years old...

when they came in the name of the Lord

No one bothered to tell his parents

They took him in the name of the Lord

He was taken to St. Elizabeth

to be raised in the name of the Lord

He was called names and he was beaten...

beaten in the name of the Lord...

Hau!
(Rest well Grandma)

CEKPA

From the Author

   When I was about 11 years old, my grandfather's niece had a set of twins. Ever since we heard that bit of news, my grandfather used to make it a point when visiting his sister, to see these boys...and he would say "which is the good one and which is the bad one?" As the twins got older he would ask them, "are you the good twin...or the bad twin?"

   Not knowing why he was asking them, I always took it as a form of teasing, until my grandmother related the story to me. The question that brought out the Cekpa story was only, "why can't people ever get along?"...I asked it under my breath, not knowing that she was listening.

   But this ritual with my grandfather continued until his death in the mid 1980's...

   Many of the stories the old ones told are life lessons...

   In our story, even though the Creator hadn't meant to directly harm his children, in a round about way that has happened. But we are ultimately responsible for our decisions, or even our indecisions.

   We have become creators of our own destiny, and we must teach our children that although the choices we make may not affect us, or those around us, today, or tomorrow...somewhere down the road, each choice we make today will affect us or those we come into contact with, and our children should know, that our choices are very important, no matter how insignificant they may seem today.

   Also in our story, before the arrival of the twins, the people lived in harmony. They worked together, they played together, and they worshipped together.

   After the twins departed then the dissention came, and the doubt about what to do, what if this?... and what if that?...but possibly the very worst seed that was planted was gossip...or rumor, and we've all seen what that one can do to families, and villages, and Nations...

   My next offering..."Cekpa"...which is Lakota for "umbilical cord" referring to "the navel", or also "twins"...

Hau!
(for Mark and Mike)

CEKPA
(The Twins...)

A Short Story
by
Eya Mani

Long long ago...before the coming of the white man, the people had lived in peace...

The creator provided enough game for hides for their shelter and for their clothing, and they had plenty of meat and a variety of small game and game birds and fish. With wild fruit and roots and herbs they dug up during the seasons, they had a variety of food... more than enough to live well, and also to provide for their medicines.

The people were happy and content and they spent a lot of time "playing", or as one would say today...they loved to pow-wow.

The people would give thanks to the creator for their good fortune, then they would sing and dance, and the children would play games and the men would gamble. The young men and boys would run foot races and horseback races and they would have contests with the bow and lance. The women would see who had made the finest quill work, with the brightest colors, the finest and strongest stitches, and who had the very finest of tanned hides.

All this was done with good intent, and because the people had such a good way of life, they started the practice of giving the very finest they had to the first person who admired their work. But this too was done in reverence to the creator and to mother earth and the many animals and plants that sacrificed so their work would be complete.

It is said that one day the creator was admiring his children and he was discussing their good nature and attitude with mother earth, and because the creator likes a good joke, he wanted to play one on his children. But mother earth was not so keen about letting the creator play jokes on her children, but he persisted so she told him that he could. But she made him promise that he would not harm her children because they had such a respect for her, and such reverence for him...then she agreed.

He said he would send them a present...the present would be the ability to choose their own destiny...to choose right from wrong, good from bad, and to make their own choices as to which road they would follow.

When mother earth heard this, she also made him promise that he would leave all decision making totally up to their children, and he would not interfere with their right to decide.

And so it was...

As his instrument, the creator made his first set of twins...of course these were not ordinary twins...they were very special twins.

Although they appeared normal in everyway, there was a difference between the two, they were the exact opposite of each other.

While one was good, kind and generous, the other was not so good, kind or generous...

You might even say the other twin was very naughty...

Although he was not bad, one might say that he was adventurous, he was always looking for attention for himself and he found it anyway he could...

The twins were told to go out and "move among the people"...but they were not to become involved with the people directly or harm the people in any way. They were only to create situations and circumstances where the people would have to choose right from wrong and good from bad.

And so, the twins set out on their first adventure...

As it happened the time was when the timpsila are harvested, and the people have a lot of work to do, that the twins blew in on a western wind. They had taken the form of "tumbleweeds", and the wind had blown them many miles before they came to a group of tipi's and they could see the people working.

The "bad twin" said he would be first and the "good twin" had to go along with him, so they took the form of an old man and an old woman. The woman was riding an old broken-down horse and the old man was leading the horse. All were in very bad condition and they had clearly seen very hard times...

When the people saw them approaching, they immediately stopped work and some started preparing a meal for their guests, others got out their finest clothing and still others brought their finest horses as gifts for their impoverished guests.

After the visitors had eaten and were given the gifts from the people, they were asked where they came from and where they were going.

The old man, knowing of the peoples love to sing and dance, told them they had heard that there was a "celebration" at such and such a place, and they had come a very great distance to attend. The celebration was to be very big and "impressive", with the playing of many games, much gambling, and everyone was assured that they would be very welcome to attend. As the old man and old woman were in a hurry to spread the word to all those they encountered, and also to get a good camp ground, they left soon after.

After the old couple had gone, the people went back to work. But some, mostly the younger people, were impressed with the news of the "big doings" and they wanted to attend. But most of the older people were not impressed.

Instead, the camp leader sent out a rider to go ask their relatives, who were also camped out along the river a few miles away, what their intent was...

The rider returned and said their brothers had decided not to attend even though their visit from the old ones had been equally impressive. Since the day of the supposed "doings" was a few days off, the two camp leaders decided to meet and discuss what their people wanted to do.

Meanwhile they had also sent out riders to the other camps along the river to bring word back about what the people were going to do about the "big doings".

On the appointed day of the celebration, two riders were again sent out to track the old couple.

The story they related was astonishing and comical...

It seems when the two riders had approached the site of the "celebration", they couldn't see anyone around, but they could hear voices, so they approached unseen.

In a clearing they saw two rather large tumbleweeds. The voices seemed to be coming from them, and they seemed to be in a heated argument.

Then right before their eyes, the two tumbleweeds became two identical twins...the first twins the two riders had ever seen...

The "bad" twin was complaining that the "good" twin had not been convincing enough to fool the people into believing that there indeed would be a pow wow. But the "good" twin, who was seated on the ground, only commented about the generosity of the people, the good food he had eaten, and he was openly admiring the people's handiwork.

But the "bad" twin threw dust into the air, and he paced back and forth telling the "good" twin that they had missed a chance to have a really good laugh, if everyone had shown up as he had expected. He went on to comment that the people would have been very angry and confused, and they would have started pointing fingers and arguing, and this and that...he was trying to get an argument out of the "good" twin.

But the "good" twin only commented that they should be on their way since no one was going to show up and be fooled...and again they turned themselves into tumbleweeds and although there was no breeze blowing, they "blew" themselves up to the riverbank and rolled themselves across the waters, up onto the opposite riverbank and on out of sight.

The twins had not left the people untouched...for they had planted the seeds of dissent, doubt, and gossip.

Next time you see a large tumbleweed on the move...know that the twins have been visiting, and only time will tell what fruits their work will bear.

Hau!

CHARLIE...

From the Author

In writing these stories and poems I hope to give the reader insight into the daily lives of my People...the tragedy, the humor, the learning lessons, and sometimes the similarities and the differences of cultures.

The story of grandma's dogs always brings to mind the place of keeping animals...

My grandfather always said that anything that you are blessed with, whether it's a dog, horses, or cattle, should be taken care of properly. Dogs are not meant to be kept chained or penned up, horses are to be treated gently and manicured regularly, and cattle are to be watched on a daily basis.

I now live in a community and I have no desire to keep dogs, because along with the keeping of dogs, we have to give them shots and keep them penned or chained.

To chain up or keep an animal penned up is to keep it 'prisoner'...I would not like to live like that, and I'm sure most people wouldn't like that experience either, yet they do these things for selfish reasons, whatever they may be.

But enough...

Let's now visit my childhood home once more, and see what grandma's dogs are doing...

My next offering...CHARLIE...

Hau!

CHARLIE...

A Short Story
By
Eya Mani

One morning after breakfast, my grandmother gathered the leftovers to take out to feed her dogs...

She had two gold colored Siberian Huskies, one male and one female, of which she was very proud, and to which she spoke the language. Some times she would comment that they understood and listened better than her children did.

This always brought a smile to my grandfather's face...and a chuckle of agreement.

She had my uncles build them a beautiful house, and sometimes they would comment that the dogs ate better, and had a better place to sleep then they did. But these comments were made in jest, and everyone was very watchful of grandma's dogs, and just as proud of them.

Every spring in her litter the female only produced one, two, or maybe three pups...and I couldn't understand why.

Weren't dogs supposed to have up to 10 pups in a litter...?

One day I asked, and my grandfather told me that the original Lakota dogs were like my grandmother's Huskies...wild...and that no one really owned them. And because they cared so much for their young, they only had one or two, and sometimes three pups...but they only had enough puppies that they could care for properly, and to ensure that their line would continue.

On this particular morning it was very cold and nippy out...but when I volunteered to take the food out to the dogs, my grandmother declined...saying she wanted to feed the dogs herself...

As she made her way to the doghouse, she pulled her shawl closer about her, noting that it was colder than usual for this time of year. As she walked, she felt at peace, and she started saying her morning prayers...hearing the snow crunch under her feet and feeling her nostril's stick together...it was good to be alive!

Since she didn't see her dogs out and about, she thought they were inside keeping warm.

She loved this time of day, she stopped to look around...very early morning...it gave her a sense of peace and she continued to say her prayers as she continued on to the dogs' home out beyond the root cellar...

When she got to the dog house she noticed no fresh tracks either going in or leaving, so she set the dish with the food in it, down in front of the blanket that covered the door, and she said, "Wanle sunka...lena yuta..." (Take this, dog...and eat...)

From inside the dog house came a voice..."Oh huh...pila mayape..." (Ok...thank you)

Still deep into her prayers...this voice from inside the doghouse shook her up...and she took a step backwards and covered her mouth with her hands...

Holding her breath she was getting ready to turn and run...but she was stopped dead in her tracks when two hands reached out from inside the doghouse, grabbed the dish and took it back inside...and before she could move, or turn and run, the right hand reached back outside the blanket and dropped a dollar bill on the ground...

She fled...

She covered the distance to the log house in nothing flat, and as she burst through the door, she was shouting..."they're alive...they're alive...they spoke to me!!! And...they gave me this!!!"...and with this outburst...she threw the dollar bill on the table.

Just for a moment everyone just stared at grandma...then at each other...and just as quickly as she had entered, the log house emptied its people out into the snow. Some of us were falling as we ran...then crawling to regain our feet...then, everyone was shouting and running towards the doghouse...

One of my uncles came out of one of the bunk houses with a 30-30, stopping on the porch, he slammed a round into the chamber and joined the chase...

Behind him the two Huskies came bounding out of the bunkhouse, then running to lead this mob...they were ready to protect their keepers if necessary...but no one paid any attention to them...everyone was too intent on the dogs who turned human...

As we neared the doghouse, the blanket that covered the doghouse door was pulled back inside, and someone came crawling out...pushing the empty plate in front of him.

This brought everyone up short...and the people in back, ran into the people in front...

Silence...no one moved...but the dogs were standing there, looking at us too...then they started jumping around the man who had crawled out of their house...pushing the empty plate...

It was cousin Charlie... from the community...

He got to his feet, straightened his clothing and looked around...trying to see why everyone had been running towards him...and one of these people was armed too!

...Charlie came forward and wiping his mouth, handed my grandmother back her plate...and he said "thank you" again...still no one moved...silence...

Then...everyone broke up into a great round of laughter...even the dogs were howling, my grandmother was laughing especially hard... she was laughing so hard she had tears in her eyes...so she covered her face with her shawl.

My grandfather was laughing so hard...he had to lean against the doghouse, and he was holding his sides...his tummy was bouncing.

Old Charlie had no idea what everyone was laughing about...but I'm sure one of them told him later...anyway. He left everyone standing there and went to get a cup of hot coffee...later, over more coffee and a proper breakfast, Charlie said he had been walking back from town, and he had gotten caught in the dark...he didn't want to bother anyone, but it had started to snow...and because it was so cold, he had asked the dogs if he could stay with them that night, and they both came out and let him in.

Charlie agreed to stay for dinner and he told us all the latest news he had heard from his travels...and after dinner, my grandparents would take him back to the community when they went to get their mail.

As they were getting ready to leave...one of my uncles said, "So Ma...what were you thinking when you saw that hand come out of the dog house and leave you a dollar...?"

...grandma said..."I was thinking...gee!...where would my dogs be getting their money...?"

After grandma and grandpa had driven off with cousin Charlie, us kids returned to our chores while the uncles prepared to leave for work...but throughout the day, the morning's events kept popping up in my head and I would burst out laughing...

Hau!

CIRCLE

From the Author

Circle is the second poem that I have written. In contrast to "Tuwa Oyake Na" which took well over two years to write, "Circle" took only a few minutes to write.

One day I was working on the family vehicle. It was very cold and windy out, and I was very miserable. Somehow I kept thinking about my grandmother and things she taught me...

After an hour outside, and being chilled to the bones, I went back inside to get a cup of coffee and warm up a bit. Seating myself at the kitchen table, I saw that someone had been reading the weekly paper and I happened to glance down at the page and there was a poetry contest.

Setting my coffee down I picked up a pen and wrote down my thoughts, which kept recurring all that miserable morning! I jotted down the poem, stuffed it in an envelope and asked my wife to mail it for me.

The Poem "Circle" won awards in 1995, 1996, 1997, and again in 1998. Unfortunately I wasn't able to attend any of the gala events and claim my prizes, but I shared my poem with a friend of mine from Colorado.

One day in March 1998 my friend from Colorado brought me this computer and told me to put my thoughts down on paper and who knows, maybe even get published?

Thanks to my friend, my dream, as well as his intentions are realized.

In 1999 I was finally able to attend the 5th Annual Famous Poets Society Convention in Reno, Nevada. I was also able to take my wife of 24 years and our son JR who was 14 at that time.

"Circle" illustrates how Lakota life has changed very little from the time of my first remembrance of picking berries with my grandmother to my adulthood and acquiring a family of my own.

The cycle continues...as I am now the grandparent and I still have to go and pick berries and roots much as my grandmother did, but for different reasons.

Hau!

CIRCLE

A Poem
by
Eya Mani

I turned around and asked,
"Why do we pick berries, Grandmother?"
"So we might live my Grandson"

I turned around and asked,
"Where have all the horses gone, Grandmother?"
"So we might live my Grandson"

I turned around and asked,
"Why must I go to school, Grandmother?"
"So you will learn to live my Grandson"

I turned around and asked,
"Why must I go away to fight, Grandmother?"
"So all might live my Grandson"

I turned around and asked,
"Now what can I do for you Grandmother?"
"Now you must go and live my Grandson"

I turned around and asked,
"Would you like to meet my son Grandmother?"
"Yes, my Grandson"

He turned around and asked,
"Why do we pick berries, Great Grandmother?"
"So we might live my Grandson"

Hau!

(miss you Grandma)

THE DEER HUNTER

From the Author

In 1992 I was on my way to Denver, Colorado with my father-in-law and one of our friends.

The time was fall and it was raining...the trip was going to be long.

We started out late in the evening so we could be in Denver the next morning. We had driven about halfway and we had been riding in silence. We must have all been thinking about the same things because one by one we started telling stories we had heard, silly stories to pass the time. The Deer Hunter is one story.

Of course the story was told in the Lakota Language and it was all the more funny. When the language is translated, some of the meaning is lost. I think I have captured the humorous intent of the story and that is what I wish to share with you. The Lakota humor. We see humor in everything, it is our way of coping with our problems or situations and it takes the edge off.

In our case, it helped the trip seem that much more enjoyable and so much shorter, and now I offer you, The Deer Hunter.

Hau!

THE DEER HUNTER

A Short Story

by

Eya Mani

The men had been standing around telling stories, funny stories, sometimes silly stories about the old times and how some of the old ones dealt with problems. Some times logic isn't always the best policy?

Anyway, they say the old one had been living alone outside the village for as long as anyone could remember. Living alone. Never bothering anyone. Never speaking to anyone. Never going to town. Forever busy. Doing things important only to him.

One day the village had a new pastor to replace the one that was retiring. It was said the new pastor knew how to speak the language, and speak it fluently too!

This meant trouble for the old one. He just knew that the new pastor would be visiting him any day now. And he was right!

The preacher came in the evening and didn't stay long. But he greeted the old one and introduced himself and asked the old one to come the next Sunday for church. There would be a village picnic and he would get a chance to meet everyone then.

The old one reluctantly agreed to be there. And so the preacher left feeling good.

When Sunday came the old one waited until the last person had gone into the church before he left his house. He wanted to find a seat in the back, way in the back where he wouldn't be noticed. He had never attended a white man's church, but he knew it would be different!

When he came in he was surprised to see everyone seated in the back. The entire back of the church was filled and the only seating he could find was way up in front. As he took his seat he knew everyone was watching.

The pastor greeted him loudly, bringing more attention to him. He didn't like that.

Just as the church services were to start, two young ladies came in and seated themselves directly in front of the old one. The pastor asked everyone to rise for opening prayer. Not knowing why everyone had stood up, the old one also stood up and looked around. Everyone had their head down and their eyes were closed. After prayer everyone was seated again, and the old one found himself wondering what he had come for. The pastor was wearing a white robe and was speaking in a language he had never heard before, but he knew it was not the white man's language!

The people were asked again to rise and again everyone had their heads down and their eyes closed. The old one was not used to this. He had prayed with his head uplifted and his arms outstretched asking for guidance and strength. He let his mind wander. He didn't know what he could let his eyes rest on but he found the young woman in front of him to be very good to look upon. He remembered his youth and such a woman!

The people were seated again. And they stood again. And again the old one let his eyes wander.

His eyes took in the smallness of the womans waist, and the roundness of her hips. His eyes came to rest on her buttocks. But this was troubling! Her dress was stuffed between her buttocks! She must be in real discomfort! Long ago, he too had known such discomfort.

The old one turned slowly around to see if anyone was watching. All were in the ashamed posture yet! He had to help her! No! He had to think about this!!

What if he did help her and someone saw? They might think badly of him. How would he live then? What would they say? Wait...he had to think...once when he was young he had such an experience! He had been hunting the very elusive white-tailed deer. He had run a great distance and now as he was getting close to his quarry, moving very slowly, hunched over with his bow and arrow at the ready. It had been bothering him for sometime now.

He had a Bite!

The leather cloth he wore had worked its way up between his buttocks and he was getting very sore, and the feeling was a burning sensation because of the sweat. Yes! She must be feeling that way by now! Very great discomfort! And she, a woman! He had to help! The people could say nothing if they knew that he was helping a woman. Could they?

The people were seated again for a time before they were asked to rise again. This gave the old one time to ponder this most important matter. He was a Lakota warrior! Protector of women and children! Keeper of the Law! At all costs. Protect the women and children from harm! The people had to understand...

The people all rose again and hung their heads and closed their eyes. With best intentions, the old one reached down and pulled out the dress material. In a flash the young woman whirled and slapped him across the face. Whack! The old one turned quickly to see if anyone had seen what had just happened. Good! No one moved an eyelid! He was safe. He had relieved her discomfort but she had reacted in a most peculiar way! Young people! He was indignant! Such thanklessness!

As he stood thinking about this he thought better of it. Maybe he should have left well enough alone? Maybe he should have left her to her discomfort? After all, she was a woman. Who can tell what a woman might think?

Without thinking about it the old one reached down and pushed the dress material back in...giving her back her bite!!!

Hau!!

GRAND RIVER

From the Author

Grand River came about after I saw one of my friends in McLaughlin, SD.

It broke my heart to see this man because as children we had been very close. I'd known him since very early childhood. He had been the catcher on our baseball team, we went to school together and he even enlisted in the Marine Corps after I did in 1969.

My friend comes from a very respectable and honorable family...but when I saw my friend, I saw a man lost and confused. He was trying to live and cope with today's problems but with the mentality of our childhood, and the pureness and the order of it, but he has clearly lost...or has he? I sometimes think he has not!

We lived our childhood at a time when everyone had mom's and dad's, grandparents and uncle's and aunt's, and everyone was glad to be related to one another, and we helped each other. We did not live in the isolationist environment we live in today.

Now everyone and everything that we had known and had loved is gone. We are on deck, with the passing of our elders, now we will be the very next to go...lets hope we leave "tracks" for our future generations to follow.

My story of Grand River is the inability of white society and white culture to change Lakota Culture. In our language there are no words to say "I Love You" or "Goodbye" and when I parted with my friend, he had to say it in English, and he made me cry, as I am while writing this short introduction.

My friend had married one of my cousins after he had gotten out of the Marine Corps, and when we had met at the clinic in McLaughlin, his wife was very ill. He did not tell me she was ill either...instead, he asked me about my own family and offered words of encouragement and humor.

A few weeks after I last saw my friend, his wife passed on...

The Lakota have long been puzzled at the white man for wanting to change anything and everything he came into contact with, and that change was usually for the worse...and my friends steadfast belief in his childhood teachings stood out very clear for me to find my way...

Hau!

GRAND RIVER

A Poem
by
Eya Mani

Wakpala...is called "the Land of Gall"
Eagle Catcher is now the Rattlesnake...
our culture in exchange for the whiteman's?...

I cannot say "I Love You"...
and we have no words that mean "Goodbye"

Rock Corral...is now Rock Creek
our home after he took the "Long Hair" down...
no one will tell us where they laid him...

still... I cannot say "I Love You"
and we have no words that mean "Goodbye"

Black Horse is still Black Horse...
all its people dead and gone...only our beloved Grand River
like our Culture will remain...

I don't need words... to say "I Love You"
...I never want to say "Goodbye"...

Hau!

IN BROAD DAYLIGHT

From the Author

"Is anyone else here crazy too?" was written as an illustration of what some Vietnam Veterans "see" and "hear"...

One of our Standing Rock Tribal Councilwomen made a comment about our Veterans, "Why do Veterans deserve preferential treatment...they aren't any better than anyone else..."

The veteran she was addressing answered her, "We aren't like you...we want to be, but we can't be like you anymore."

In visiting with my counselor today I came to realize that a lot of our Veterans "see" and "hear" things...but whatever they see or hear, they are not like anyone else, and they are different...

After my return from Viet Nam my father asked me if I ever experienced anything like this and I said "no" without thinking about it. He passed on in 1984 so I never had the opportunity to discuss any of this with him.

He told me he always saw a "green frog." This was usually on his chest and he couldn't get rid of it until he did what he was "supposed to do?", I am still at a loss at what he meant by that. But I am sure I will understand it some day.

Two Veterans told me of their "experiences" that occur regularly, this story is an attempt to illustrate some of what I was told.

It is not an analysis by any means, only a relation of what some have experienced, and I still do not know nor can I interpret the meanings of these experiences. Only through sharing our experiences will we come to understand what they truly mean. As my counselor said, "This is only the tip of the iceberg and our consciousness is very, very deep and it goes back for generations."

If there are any other Veterans out there who have had these kinds of experiences, take heart, you are not crazy...but we are not like anyone else.

My next offering...In Broad Daylight.

Hau!

IN BROAD DAYLIGHT
(Anyone else here crazy?)

*An Observation
by
Eya Mani*

The man had been uneasy all morning...he had gotten up before his usual time of 0400 hrs...and he had spent his time making coffee, drinking cup after cup and smoking as many cigarettes.

He was now pacing the floor, going from window to window...watching...waiting.

They were coming and he knew it...and he knew this time it would be different too!

They always came with the light, either before daylight or at twilight, but they were never here in broad daylight before...he just knew they would be here soon even though the sun had been up for over an hour now.

Now...they were late...and he didn't like it...and he was getting more nervous and edgy as the minutes went by...

He was alone in the big house. He preferred it this way. He had children but they were grown now and they had their own to think about. But it didn't matter who was around, ...when they came they came...they didn't care who he was with...and they didn't care where he was either. That was the scary part...

He had seen them first in his nightmares, or in his drunken sleep. But now they had come alive and he saw them as plain as anyone in real time, and they usually stayed in that time before true daylight, before darkness and light, and when the sun would appear they would also disappear...usually.

He didn't know how...but he knew it would be different this time.

He never spoke with them when they came...but he could read their thoughts...and they could read his mind too, if he let them, and that's what was so scary about it.

He knew they wouldn't harm him...at least he didn't think they would harm him...but when they came for him...they never let him know why either...but they always asked the same question, which was more of an order.

"You ready? let's go chief, time to go, they sent us for you, we have to be getting back...next time we come you better be ready...okay chief...?"

He never answered them when they came and tried to get him to converse with them...

He was afraid they would take him with them, and he didn't know where they wanted to take him or where they came from, but he knew he didn't want to go with them...

His mind drifted...suddenly.

THERE!!!...they were coming...how did they know...how did they know...?

The point man first...he was just rounding the first bend in the road...skirting the woods and brush...stopping and kneeling...waiting...hand signals...coming to the first house, flat against the walls, checking his corners, first a quick peek, then a more easy look, then the hand signals again...he wasn't alone...with faces painted and in full combat dress...they were coming for him...a killer team...

Why was a killer team coming for him...?

A car drove past him but the team leader didn't know it was there...why?

They could see the house but not the car? why?how?

The second man came up next before the first man moved on...checking his corners and moving on to the next house, coming closer. They always found him...he couldn't hide...he must have tried that a thousand times before...but they always found him.

The man in the house moved away from the window so they wouldn't see him...but he knew they would find him anyway...they always did, and what did they want from him?

When they arrived he could see them through the walls of the house...

The point man asked again, "You ready chief? we gotta go now! they sent us for you, we got to be getting back now..."

He wouldn't let them in this time either...but he could see them...the second man took up a position across the road, the third man went to keep watch around the rear of the house and he knelt down by the corner, ready.

But ready for what?

He knew if he ignored them and didn't answer them they would leave after a few minutes or so...so he tried to keep his mind a blank...but he couldn't so he prayed...

After a few interrogatories without a reply, the man said they would be back again...and they left as they had come.

This time a dog was moving past them and it turned to snap at one of the men, only the man didn't seem to notice the dog as it snarled at him and snapped at him again...why?

After the killer team had gone, the man sat down quietly, but he was afraid, so he got to his feet on shaking legs.

Exhausted...drained...shaking...he walked outside and sat down on the porch, then he lit his last cigarette, watching the smoke rise in the cool morning air.

Damn those guys...

Why didn't they leave him alone, he just wanted to be left alone...was he the only crazy one around here?

The second sighting took place in a completely different place and under different circumstances...

The first time he had seen the warrior he was in Vietnam. He had taken all the precautions, took his pills religiously, but he caught malaria anyway...and now he was in the Army hospital at Cam Rahn Bay.

He was in bed on the second floor...his bed was facing the South China Sea...

At first he couldn't believe his ears...the unmistakable sound of a horse breathing hard...blowing hard through his nose...snorting. And the swishing sounds of the horse's feet as he moved around on the sand...

Turning to face the direction from where the sound came...the wall seemed to become transparent...invisible...then he saw the warrior sitting on the paint...saw the horse's hoofs kicking up the sand as the warrior rode along the beach...the paint was prancing from side to side, leather thong hanging from its mouth...at first on the dry sand which made the swishing sound...then on to the wet sand made wet from the lapping waters.

The warrior had on moccasins and leather leggings, his upper body was covered halfway with a robe of some sort...either buffalo or bear, but it was big and shaggy, and it left one arm exposed...

This was a powerful man, this warrior...he had thought.

The warrior's hair was tied on one side and hanging loose on the other side. In his right hand he held a lance that rested on his right foot as he rode in. Two eagle feathers and some horsehair ties hung from his lance, and a shield hung on his left arm with scalps hanging from it.

This warrior gave the strong impression of someone ready for battle...

The sick man tried to see the warriors face as the warrior approached, but he had no face...only a dark area, as if shadowed.

The warrior rode in close just below the man's bed, and the paint moved around as the warrior sat looking up at the sick man...expectant.

Finally after a few minutes, the warrior asked, "Are you ready... grandson?"

The sick man gave no reply...he was sick and afraid...but again the question...and again he gave no reply...no words were spoken, only thoughts passing between them...

"I have to go now, but maybe next time you will be ready...?" then he was gone.

The sick man didn't even see him leave...although he was looking right at him...then the man was asleep.

The man in the bed never told anyone about what he had seen...or thought he had seen, because they would have thought him crazy...maybe he had dreamed it?

But with the things that were happening around him, he soon forgot about the warrior on the paint horse. All that was left of that experience was the overwhelming feeling of peace...calm...strength and courage.

The warrior visited him again many years later...

The warrior came riding up from the south, it was evening and the man was sick in bed from malaria again, when the warrior came riding up.

He stopped outside the mans window and again the paint was prancing in place...

The warrior's dress was the same, only this time the shield was slung over his left shoulder... resting more on his back...but he still had no face.

The man wasn't afraid of the warrior. Instead, he felt humble that one so great should come to see him again...but he was puzzled why he should come when he was so sick...

Again the question, "Are you ready grandson...?" and again he did not reply...

Again the question, "Are you ready grandson?"

This time the man in the bed answered..."No grandfather, I am not ready yet..."

The warrior turned the paint and the went west over the hill...before the warrior rode out of sight, he heard "When I come again for you...maybe you will be ready then...?"

The man who was sick in bed recovered quickly after that visit, and he was never bothered by the reoccurrence of malaria again...but he was to be visited one last time by this great warrior riding his war horse...

The warrior's paint was prancing from side to side, keeping up with the fast moving car on the interstate.

He was on the opposite side of the road, riding along the fence, and the man knew he was there without looking…

The warrior rode with him in silence for a few miles then asked, "Are you ready now grandson…?"

This time the man in the car answered out loud…"No, I am not ready yet grandfather."

The paint and the warrior stayed with him a few more miles riding in silence and then he was gone…

After the warrior left him, the man driving the car knew he didn't have any more worries…

He knew exactly what had to be done and how he was going to get it done…he knew help was only a prayer away.

But first, he would stop in the Black Hills that night and see his brother, share a beer with him and then go on to his own home…

…he turned up the radio and sang along…

Hau!

INDIAN COUNTRY

From the Author

In 1969 five of my family embarked on a journey unlike any other. What we were to experience would shape our lives and those of our friends, acquaintances, family, and our future generations. All are still struggling to deal and come to terms with our experience.

My Brother Joe, my Uncle Conrad Lee, my Cousin Owen, my Cousin Georgie and I were to experience "hell on earth". Georgie was shot twice, and Conrad Lee was KIA in September of 1970. He had just turned 17 years old at that time, the rest of us had just turned 20.

Casualties of war. The participants, our families, our marriages, our children and our grandchildren. We are still trying to put our lives back together again, and it is very difficult.

As my brother puts it. "Who gives a damn?"

Many of us suffer from Alcoholism, and our children and grandchildren are born with Spina Bifida...cancer...or mentally retarded. And our Government refused to face the truth...we were poisoned by our own Government, and they will not acknowledge that truth!

As I write this, my son Timothy has joined the US Navy, and my oldest son plans on joining the US Army. Leaving only our youngest son who is now 14 years old.

My experience has strengthened my Faith in my God, but my body is suffering from effects of our living conditions while in Viet Nam.

Once, while standing security for our men as they filled the company's canteens with river water, I went upstream 50 meters from the detail. I found bodies bloated...floating in the water along the shore...oozing blackened bodies...body fluids draining from decaying flesh into the water.

I said nothing of this to the men. I only made sure they put Halizone tablets in each and every canteen before drinking.

When I drank water from my canteens, I had to hold my breath...and I tried to think of better times.

Those of us who have experienced combat first hand relive these episodes on a nightly, or a daily basis, time and time again. My therapy is to stay away from conflict, arguments, politics, large crowds, and loud sudden noises. And I write about my experience and now I can talk about it...though not all the time.

With the Lords help. I will be whole again...and now I offer you "Indian Country."

Hau!

INDIAN COUNTRY
(Enemy Territory...Indian Reservations)

A Short Story
by
Eya Mani

The man had fallen into a troubled sleep...

Whup! Whup! Whup!...

...the huge rotors of the CH-53 beat the air, slowing the decent of the aircraft carrying the Marines into battle...the man was on the second '53 coming into a hot landing zone, seated right across the gangway was the Company Commander.

Grim...everyone was looking very grim...

Usually only one "bush company" was allowed in the rear at any one time, but his company, Golf Company 2nd Battalion 7th Marines, had been recalled early to resupply with Hotel 2/7 at Battalion Headquarters, LZ Baldy, I-Corps, Republic of Viet Nam.

The word was...they were on a "Reactionary Force" to help Hotel out of an ambush they had walked into along the Thu Bon River. They had been called out a day earlier than expected and the severity of the situation was compounded by the impromptu "Sacrament of the Last Rights" performed as the men were saddlingup.

Every man was issued extra ammunition...

He remembered the first time he had seen her. It was after his family had moved home from the big city and he was in the third grade...and there she was...nothing to look at really...just a scrawny little skinny kid with very big eyes and her hair was thin.

He remembered because he had felt sorry for her...mostly because everyone made fun of her...and his people said she was "no good" because she was a half-breed and she came from a "bad family". But he was too young to know of such things so he stuck up for her.

He remembered he had gotten into a fist fight with a 5th grade boy because he had been teasing her and had made her cry...so he waited after school for the older kids to get out of school, then he whipped the 5th grader real good...but she wasn't there to see him do it...because she had been chased home by some of the other kids.

When everyone in the small village had heard what he had done, no one ever bothered her again.

The huge aircraft shuddered and he saw a large hole appear between his feet. When he looked up he could see the sky through the exit hole made in the ceiling...the round had narrowly missed the hydraulic lines running the length of the aircraft.

After his fight with the 5th grader, even the 6th grade boys made room for him when he came around. He always had a team to be on and he was always chosen first when teams were playing.

And "she" was always there to cheer him and his team on. She brought him pop and candy from her home, things she always had...and he seldom got...because that's the way her parents were...they never had time for her but they gave her things...probably their way to show affection...this he knew about.

As they grew older she continued to follow him around, always making it a point to be next to him at any event they both were attending. She had even made friends with his female cousins so she could be close to him.

One day he asked his uncle Ray about her and the way she treated him...and uncle Ray simply said, "You're her hero, she feels safe around you, she trusts you...don't ever betray that trust."

But as they both grew up, he was growing uncomfortable being around her so much...

These new feelings he couldn't talk about...with anyone.

The gunfight was into its second day now, and they were taking a lot of sniper fire from high up on the cliffs that were on both sides of the river. They too were caught in ambush with Hotel Company.

He had called in artillery and air strikes which didn't seem to be doing any good...the enemy was dug in too deep.

That evening he had gone with his Company Commander across the river to have a "face to face" with Hotel's Company Commander. As they were crossing the river after dark, he remembered how terrified he had been, but he had also remembered that it was possibly the calmest he had ever been.

"Is this how it is before you die?"

A nurse sat astraddle of him, hands on his shoulders shaking him violently, screaming, crying, shouting...."wakeup! don't go to sleep! get up! don't go to sleep!!!", now slapping him hard, then pushing up and down on his ribs, as if she were trying to restart his breathing, but he just wanted to go home...he was so very tired.

One day he had gone into town to spend the weekend with his cousin...and she was there.

While his aunts and uncles were playing cards upstairs, he and his cousins were in the basement playing monopoly, when she suggested they play "hide and seek".

They were both the same age, but she didn't look like his female cousin, who was two years older. Instead she was 'round' and she was very pleasant to look at.

Her big eyes had grown up with her as well as some of her other 'parts', and he felt uncomfortable around her all the time now.

The man came violently awake, heaving over the side of the hospital bed, he let fly a large blood clot that had formed in his stomach...he had been bleeding internally...and with this release, the nurse who had been sitting on him was thrown to the floor, but she stood up laughing and crying at the same time, just as the doctors and other nurses burst through the door.

The mans i.v.'s were reattached and the icepacks were taken away...then after an examination and a sponge bath, he was allowed to go to sleep, but the little nurse who he had so violently pitched to the floor, insisted on staying at his bedside until all danger had passed.

He fell very quickly into a fitfull sleep...

His father's younger brother was with Hotel 2/7 and they visited from time to time and exchanged war stories whenever they could, or when they had a chance to drink a few beers together.

While the Captains were making plans, his uncle had introduced him as his 'cousin' to the men in his squad.

His uncle also told him of the news back home and he said that his "friend" was said to be in the ranks of one of the oldest professions on earth..."and I don't mean that she's a farmer neither!" was the way he had put it. Everyone who heard his comment had a good laugh, but he later remembered feeling very sad to hear that bit of news.

He never got one letter from her, but he knew why...

At midnight his company went up the cliffs on their side of the river, and Hotel went up the cliffs on the other side. They met no resistance and at dawn a thorough search of the area turned up no clues as to who had been there or how many there were.

Not one casing from an expended round had been found...not even a foot print.

This was indeed a formidable enemy...

Not knowing who they were fighting or how many, the Marines were in real danger...

And they were to learn the battle was far from being over...

She had chosen him to be the first 'seeker...' and he was to remain in the basement and count to 100 while the others ran outside to hide.

After the wounded had been evacuated and the company had been resupplied, the men expended their excess ammunition into the jungle.

This in itself was awesome...trees and foliage that would have been hard to penetrate, had been cleared away in a few minutes...their firepower was truly awesome.

But he also knew that this show of firepower was as much a warning, just in case the enemy was there watching...and he knew they were watching.

Standing on the opposite riverbank, his uncle had been waving. When he waved back, he
could hear the shout, "Waonchiglaka"..."Take care of yourself"...then he was gone.

The man stirred fitfully and came awake...startled...fearful...sweating.

The nurse applied a wet towel to his barechest and forehead to keep him cool...and as he closed his eyes again she whispered "sssssshhhhh...I'm here...you'll be fine...I'm here...I'll take care of you...I promise...there, there now...sssssshhhhh..."

When he had finished counting and had uncovered his eyes, she was standing right in front of him...she had put her finger to his lips to keep him quiet, then she started to undress him...

He fought her at first...then he quit...something was stirring in him...but he knew this was not the way he had imagined or had wanted it to happen...

"Not this way!!!" he had whispered in her ear...

"What's wrong?"..."Don't you want me?"..."I've been saving myself for you...and you don't want me?"..."Please!!!"..."Come back!"..."Please come back, I'm sorry..."

Without another word he had climbed the stairs and he was standing outside before he realized it...leaving her standing there crying, sobbing uncontrollably, unable to take her breath.

He could have handled it better. She would have done anything he wanted...she would

have waited for him if he'd asked her...

He gave an anguished cry and the nurse came close..."sssshhhhh...I'm here...I'll take care of you...I promise..."

He was in the second platoon, second squad with the Captain...they had been on the trail for almost two hours when...with an explosion and a metallic roar...the jungle came alive...

The point man had tripped a "daisy chain", and the booby trap had taken out the entire squad in front of him...this was followed immediately with intense automatic small weapons fire...and smoke, explosions and debris filled the air...he didn't have time for fear...but he knew anger...and anger took over.

He couldn't hear the gunfire...or the screaming ...or the cursing...

He just reloaded magazine after magazine, firing as he moved towards the enemy...firing, re-loading, moving forward, reloading and firing, moving forward...

Then it was over...as if everyone had run out of ammunition at the same time...and everyone seemed to be holding their breath...fearing they would draw more fire if they made any noise...but he had his fist clenched towards the heavens and he was cursing and screaming, "take me you son of a bitch...go on!!!! take me!!!...I'm one mean son of a bitch myself!!...come on!!...take me..."

Then he was on his knees crying, sobbing, his chest heaving, great torrents of tears coming and he was begging forgiveness for his blasphemy...praying only to be taken home safely...out of this hell...and to be allowed to live!

He heard his name...someone was calling him..."Chief"..."I'm over here Chief..."

He went to his buddy and found him lying on his back, facing up, seemingly untouched by all the hot metal that had just been expended...but his buddy didn't move...so he knelt down and lit a smoke for him... then picking up his buddy he felt the blood oozing from the many wounds the booby trap had made...shredding his young body...leaving only his face and head untouched.

His buddy asked him "Chief, don't let me die...there are so many things I haven't done yet...please...don't let me die like this..."

All he could do was hold his friend...and try not to show emotion.

The man sat bolt upright!...the nurse had to push him back down. "Shhhhhhhh!, take it easy, you're going to be alright now, sssshhhhh, I'll take care of you...I promise...I promise..."

The man realized he knew exactly when his uncle had been killed...causing his anger and his blasphemy...but he also knew he was forgiven...and he knew he would be allowed to live.

He also knew he had to find his "friend...", and ask her forgiveness as well...after all, uncle Ray would have wanted it that way...

...but he knew...he never would.

Hau!

(for Conrad Lee)

INDIAN GIRL

From the Author

   United Tribes International Pow Wow 1999 marks the 25th year since I have attended this gathering of Nations.

   Our oldest daughter and our oldest son were both attending College in UTTC, so we had a place to stay for our brief visit. As my wife and I were reminiscing about our last Pow Wow many years ago, she remembered that we had gone to see the movie "Jaws", and that I had sat up screaming in the middle of the night. She asked what I had been dreaming about, but I could not remember because it was so long ago! But we had a good laugh anyway.

   On this morning I arose early and went to breakfast, then I went to the camping area to see the camp come to life. For me this is an interesting time of day, early morning, early morning people, doing early morning things. Looking for coffee, using the portapotties, some looking for children, others just visiting with someone they have never met before.

   I said my prayers and returned to my daughter's home and later returned to the Arena area and sat with the Veterans and made small talk. As they were announcing for the 1:00 pm Grand entry a group of young ladies passed us by and got in line. One young lady turned and for a brief moment our eyes met and I could see a lifetime in that glance.

   I wish her well, and her family also.

   Her outfit was exquisite...made of satin...Bald Eagles positioned just so on the shawl and on her beaded boots...and the beadwork was phenominal...blending and coming to life with each movement of its owner.

   I beg the readers forgiveness at my humble attempts at trying to describe what I feel as I try to make my experience come to life for you...if my small offering does not take you there...then...I guess you had to be there.

And now...I give you "INDIAN GIRL"

Hau!

INYAN MNI

From the Author

The Lakota believe that all life is a circle. The white mans says "dust to dust and ashes to ashes" and this is true, but he cuts it off there. It must be included that even as we die and return to mother earth, our passing brings new life to this earth and also to her inhabitants, and it must be explained that sometimes if we are lucky, good enjoyable experiences will reoccur in our own lifetimes.

Sometime in ones life, there is a time when that experience is brought out and an example is given, such as in "Inyan Mni". And the true station of man is shown, and if that man or woman is paying attention, the experience is truly humbling.

The following story is about such an experience...a passage from boyhood to manhood, and life after that...

But others also have a version of the so-called 'indian test of manhood'...

A friend of mine once made a comment, that she would be afraid of allowing any of her sons to "go thru the ceremony."

Curious, I asked what ceremony? Her response was, "Why, making the children walk barefoot 50 miles through a desert, making them choose between a bowl of ashes and a bowl of food to teach them to fast, and the practice of making them run a gauntlet in order to teach them pain..."

I was shocked...

I had no idea that 'true Indians' had to go through such rigorous treatment!!

Why...even the Marines don't treat their own in such barbaric fashion!!!

But what surprised me was that this person was from California...and these almost identical sentiments were echoed by another of my friends who lives on the east coast!!

I quickly told my friend that to be Lakota was a 'way of life' and not a test of pain, or hunger, or stamina...but a way of life that included being grateful to the Almighty on a daily basis with a verbal address to him. And the Lakota in no way mistreated their children, and for that matter, I can say I know of no other Native American Tribe who mistreats their young...only the white man.

This I have seen first hand and it is appalling to say the least!

There is more to being Lakota than most people realize…

Much thought is taken before decisions are made…patience is taught at a very early age…sharing, helping, being polite and respectful…all these are just little parts of the whole.

So with that…I hope you enjoy the following relation of a passage from boyhood to manhood…now my next offering…"INYAN MNI"…

Hau!

INYAN MNI

A Short Story
by
Eya Mani

The man sat cleaning the old .22 rifle, although the boy had never seen him use it before, he sat and watched him clean it and wipe it down with 3in1 oil.

The family had been out at the old place for a few weeks now, and although they never usually ran out of food, now they were out of meat, and although his grandfather and his other uncles usually did all the hunting, he knew this uncle was about to go hunting, very soon.

The boys knew where all the deer usually could be found, because they use to go out everyday and stay out till after dark, playing along the river, the draws and the creeks around the home place.

Their favorite game...was to get up before daybreak and leave the house very quietly, and go sit on the highest hill overlooking the White Shirt and Hump Creeks. From this vantage point, they could watch the deer come out of the river after having had their early morning water, and find a place to bed down for the day. Then after breakfast, the boys would go back and see who could come closest to the deer without being detected...

Bringing home their first kill was a ritual that was long in the family, but that was usually accorded the boys when they reached the age of 12 or 13. These boys were still too young for that, but they could accompany the hunters while they went out, and they would learn all there was to being successful in the hunt...

While the young boy sat watching his uncle prepare the weapon, he remembered he had accompanied his uncle Reno on a hunt up by the old coal mine. His uncle had seemed to have a sixth sense, and when he went out, everyone knew there would be a feast when he returned...

His uncle Reno never spoke when they went out...he just did, and the boys observed.

On this particular hunt, his uncle had left the wagon and horses tethered a good mile and a half from his intended area of coverage. They went silently from draw to draw, from bush to bush...stopping often...squatting down...never making a sound...never making an outline of themselves...staying always within the cover of the tree line.

Just below the old coal mine there was a fork in the draw, and when they reached that point, they very silently backtracked and came over the hill from the south, so they would be going right into the thickest part of the south fork in the middle of the draw...

He remembered...they had crawled on their stomachs, starting from about midway up the hill, and on up over the top, never breaking the horizon with their outlines, this was most important...

They continued to crawl on down into the draw until they had once again entered the tree line...at this point, his uncle quietly loaded one round into the chamber of the rifle he carried...and he got slowly to his feet.

Suddenly...with a great cry...he charged headlong into the thicket...firing as he ran.

One...two...three shots...the boy had never hunted with his uncle Reno before, so he didn't know what to expect when this happened...but he also jumped to his feet...and ran screaming into the thicket.

By the time the boy had reached the bottom of the draw, his uncle was kneeling down by a very large and beautiful mule deer buck. His uncle quickly cut the animal's throat, then he ran on to a second, smaller mule deer buck which lay thrashing in the brush. His uncle also cut this animal's throat, then he turned them so their heads would be facing downhill, presumably to let them bleed freely.

The young boy remembered how this all had made him feel...cold...shivering...excited and exalted...he remembered, and a shiver ran through him again.

On their way home the young boy kept looking at his uncle. And his uncle seemed to sense the unasked question, and he answered the unasked question with..."I don't fool around!"

The man and the two boys left the house before daylight, going directly to one of the rocky buttes that lined the White Shirt Creek. After climbing this largest of the rocky buttes, they went immediately to its eastern edge...just as the sun was coming up...just as his uncle had planned.

This uncle was a different kind of hunter...and although he planned and shared his intentions with his company...he was a "noisy" hunter.

Below the rim rock were trees and thick brush which grew in patches all along the rocky butte, until here, at the south end, the butte and hills formed a short, shallow draw with very thick brush and trees.

His uncle encouraged the boys to throw rocks and stones into the brush, and to talk if they wanted too. His philosophy was to let the deer know you are coming, and to "give 'em a chance to get away..."

The trio circled the butte and found themselves back where they had started, when his uncle told them, "you boys go on ahead...I have to take a leak here...", so the two boys continued on.

As his uncle was finishing his business, a large mule deer buck jumped out from below where his uncle was standing, and his uncle said quietly..."...there he goes..."

The boys turned and watched the mule deer bound away..."like a bouncing ball...and it was going to get away..." he had thought.

His uncle calmly threw a round into the chamber and watched a second or two longer, then he raised the rifle to his shoulder...firing almost immediately.

The report and echo of the round traveling through the trees could be heard...followed by a sickening 'thud' as the round hit its mark, but the buck didn't even stumble.

His uncle cleared his throat...then he reloaded another round into the chamber, waited for another few seconds...then he raised the rifle and fired.

The second round traveled a bit further and this time there was no sound when the bullet impacted, but the huge mule deer buck tumbled and lay still...

The two boys ran to where the deer lay, in a patch of buck brush...then while his cousin bled the buck, the other boy turned to watch his uncle, who was now unloading his rifle...

Looking back to see where his uncle was standing, he was sure that the small calibre rifle wouldn't kill at that range. But as his uncle approached he said, "I was gonna let him run further, but he would have gone over the hill, you gotta give 'em a chance to get away...remember that..."

The man parked the pickup truck on the hilltop, then he sat quietly before he got out of the truck.

The man told his son, "I came here once...a long time ago...now I would like to show you something...ready?"

The man told his wife they would be within sight all the way down to where they would be going, and they would wave when they were ready, then he and their son left.

The man carried a .22 magnum and his son carried a .22 Ruger automatic carbine, but he didn't want to shoot anything...he was expecting his son to do that.

As they approached the rocky butte, the man told his son about the hunt he had come on with his uncle so many years ago..."and this is where he stood and took a leak, and just below there was where the deer jumped out and ran that way..."

The man felt a little disappointed that a huge mule deer buck didn't jump out, just as one had done so long ago...but he didn't let on.

He just continued around the butte with his son, taking in the sights more than anything...and he was pointing out landmarks and telling his son stories.

When they came back to where they had started, the man had a need to relieve himself, so he told his son to go on ahead...

Standing where his uncle had stood many years ago, he was lost in thought and prayer, when he heard his son whisper, "Dad, there's a buck down there..."

The mans heart leaped in his chest... "YES..."

The man told his son to be careful and watch his backdrop, but his son was already raising the rifle.

The mule deer must have moved, because his son ducked and ran along the rim 30 feet or so and stopped, and raised the rifle again.

Remembering his uncle's words, the man raised his rifle and fired a shot into the hillside, scaring the mule deer into a run, giving him a chance to get away...

The man watched as the mule deer came bounding out of the trees...the man could see it was a young buck, two year old.

The shot and the sound of the round traveling along the trees, then the dull 'thud' brought shivers, but almost immediately the second shot was heard and the man saw the buck tumble and fall exactly where the older buck had fallen so many years ago...and his heart was both sad...and glad.

As they field-dressed the young buck and his son took his first taste of fresh kill liver, the man said a prayer of thanks and gratitude...and he remembered.

Hau!

LAKOTA HOKSILA

From the Author

    Lakota Hoksila is a story in answer to a question I once posed to my Grandmother on why certain songs were sung and the stories behind them.

    In all likelihood the story is true... but I leave that up to the reader.

    ...when telling a story, there are many things to remember...

    Lakota never named anyone in their stories unless naming would add to the story.

    Anonymity is a sign of respect...rather they would relate the story and the listener had to figure out who and what.

    There are many songs that are sung in Honor of someone who has done a great service for the People...most of these can be heard at Pow Wows or Honoring Ceremonies.

    And now...my next offering..."Lakota Hoksila."

Hau!

LAKOTA HOKSILA
(Indian Boy)

A Short Story
by
Eya Mani

The young boy stood watching the team of horses pull the wagon around the bend in the road. His father and his grandfather were going after another load of wood. He wished he had gone with them as they bumped along the river bed looking for newly fallen trees.

As he stood watching, he could hear his grandmother singing a new song he didn't recognize. She sang it softly, as if singing it too herself, but he knew the words and he asked her the meaning of such a song. Who was it made for? And what did this person do to have such a grand song made about him and his deeds?

His grandmother was cleaning the graves in the family cemetery as she sang, but she stopped and told him she would explain to him at lunch time. The boy got down on his knees and started pulling weeds as if each weed was a minute less he would have to wait to hear the story.

After they had eaten lunch and the men sat back to rest and visit. His grandmother took him aside into the shade of the old church and they sat down upon an old canvas tarp she had spread on the ground.

As his grandmother began the story, the boy lay down on his back so he could look up and watch the clouds. As his grandmother told the story, he would imagine the clouds forming shapes to go along with the story...

This one would be hard though, because this was a story about the cowboy who fed the people!

"Not so long ago when the government settled the reservations and told the Lakota where they could live. We moved here and the government said it was ours to own."

" Some people planted gardens, and some people raised cattle and horses, and some people went to school or the service, and others went to work for the farmers and ranchers who lived around here."

"This is a story about one of those who went to work for the farmers and ranchers who live around here."

"It wasn't long after the settlement that a great hunger came to live with the people… those who had, shared with those who didn't have, and those who knew how, did what they could to help those who couldn't…everyone did what they could to help the people in this bad time."

"All the wild game left the country or died off and the Lakota were very hungry, even the fish were not the best."

"The government had promised that the Lakota would get rations once a month in town, and so it was that we were in to get our rations when we heard the news."

"It seems a town 5 or 6 days journey, had invited all the cowboys and those people from our village who could attend, to a big rodeo and doings, and they would provide a camping grounds, fresh water and feed for the horses, and the people of the town would also share their food with the Lakota."

"All were excited that they had friends from so far away, and they didn't even know it!"

"It was decided that the young men would ride in the rodeo, but they would not ride to win, but only to put on a good show for their new friends in this far away town."

"And so the people started off…whoever had a team and wagon, or horses to ride, and some even walked alongside the wagons."

"But they sang and told stories and the women made things to give as gifts, and to trade with their new friends."

"But some of the people were not so excited, and were afraid, because they remembered what they had done to our people in the land of Red Cloud…and still, others did not trust the people from the town…but they went anyway."

"When they were within sight of the town, they sent riders out to tell them they had arrived."

"But when they were asked how many had come? And they said, 'our entire village', it was the towns people's turn to be afraid."

"The people from the town didn't come out of their homes, but looked out of the windows, and you could see that they were very afraid."

"But the Lakota were very hungry and tired…and they didn't know why their friends were afraid of them when they had invited them."

"And since nothing was offered to them, they went into the town to trade and bring back food for all to share."

"The young men, seeing that they were offered nothing as was promised, had a change of heart…"

"They asked that the rodeo be started on the next day, and they would ride to win, and then they could go home victorious."

"Among them was a young cowboy from Montana, he was a loner who had come to live with the People… and they say he liked it here."

"While these young men of the village were making plans, he was off by himself, but you could see he was in deep thought."

"The rodeo started the next morning, but the young men could not ride as well as they thought, because of their hunger…and many of them fell from the horses many times."

"Only the young man from Montana did well in the bareback and the saddle bronc, but now it was time to wrestle the steers…"

"Many of the young men tried again, but because of their hunger, none of them did well…"

"Now if you have ever seen a steer wrestler, you would know that the wrestler jumps off the horse and comes down between the horse and the steer, at full gallop."

"And he grabs the steer by the horns, and turns the steers head away from his body, and in this way, the steer falls and the cowboys wins!"

"But now it was time for the young man from Montana to wrestle the steers."

"Now before the steer wrestling began, he had come to the old people and told them to get their knives ready, for today they would have meat!"

"When the young man from Montana was ready, he let out a big war hoop as his signal for the people to get their knives ready…and for the cowboys to let loose the steer!"

"All the people were watching in silence, and the Lakota were wondering how he would do what he said he would do."

"But the young man from Montana lost no time…"

"His horse was beside the steer, then he was in the air, but when he jumped the steer he didn't come down between the animals, but instead, he went clear over the steer…and no one knows what happened because it happened too fast…and there was much dust and dirt in the air!"

"But they say that he popped the steers neck!"

"Some say you could hear it crack way over yonder where the wagons were."

"Whatever happened, the young man from Montana wasn't given another chance that day...but he was told he could try again on the next day."

"But the people had meat, and they sang all night, and told funny stories, and they had a good time."

"On the second day of the rodeo, the young men rode a lot better, and a lot of them had a chance of winning."

"Even the steer wrestlers did better, but again before it was his turn, the young man from Montana came to the old people, and he told them to get their knives ready, for today they would again have meat!"

"Again, the people watched in silence when it was time for the young man from Montana to wrestle his steer."

"Again he gave a loud war hoop, and the cowboys let the steer out from the chute!"

"But this time, you could hear everyone take a deep breath, because the steer which came out of the chute was much bigger than the one the young man from Montana had killed yesturday!"

"But again the horse lost no time, and again the young man was in the air and this time you could see what he did!"

"As he went over the steer and grabbed the steer by the horns you could see him struggle for just a second, and then in one quick motion his feet came down and the steer came over the top of him, and you could hear the steers neck pop...and again you could hear the crack of it way back over where the wagons stood..."

"There was an outcry from the towns people, but the Lakota were cheering!"

"Never had this thing been done before..."

"And two times now..."

"The carcass was given to the Lakota but some people from the town didn't like it, they said the young man from Montana had now killed these two steers on purpose. And they didn't want him to kill anymore of their cattle."

"After much talking and explaining it was decided the young man from Montana could take part in the last days activities...even the steer wrestling, for surely he couldn't kill the biggest and the best steer the towns people had...could he?"

"That night the people feasted and told funny stories and laughed, and everyone was filled with the meat of the fallen steer."

"And oh! Such meat!"

"Never had so much been done by one person, for so many!"

"And the people gave thanks and invited the towns people to come and join in the celebration."

"And so it was that the people from the town and the Lakota who they had invited became friends."

"But there was still one more day of rodeo left, and the towns people let it be known, that the biggest steer would be saved for the young man from Montana, and now betting was taking place over who would win the contest, the steer or the young man from Montana!"

"On the final day of the rodeo the young men again changed their minds and some of them won and some of them lost. They did this because they had now become friends with the townspeople. But everyone waited for the steer wrestling to begin. And the young man from Montana would wrestle his steer last."

"Now the steer that the young man from Montana was supposed to wrestle was kept apart in a separate pen, and some went to look at this fine animal...their next meal!"

"But when they saw him, they were afraid."

"They say that his horns spread out as wide as a man was tall...and when you looked into those eyes...oh... such anger!"

"They came back and told the young man from Montana, and they warned him not to try to wrestle this steer, because it would surely kill him instead!"

"The young man from Montana said nothing, but instead moved away from everyone, as was his custom, and you could see he was in very deep thought."

"Some say he was praying because he was afraid."

"And then some say he was just being like he always was, a loner."

"Still others said he was asking for the strength to do for the people what he said he would do..."

"This time before the steer wrestling started, he didn't tell the old ones to sharpen their knives, instead when he came to them, he said he would do whatever it was that was in their hearts."

"Now he was ready to go fight the steer..."

"When it was time, the young man from Montana showed up on his horse...but there was something wrong...he wasn't wearing his cowboy clothing...he was dressed as in the old way...as if going into battle!"

"Even his horse was stripped of all the cowboy gear."

"No saddle, no bridle, no blanket...only a leather thong was in the horse's mouth as in the old way..."

"The young man from Montana let out a very loud war hoop, and the steer was turned loose...again you could hear the people take in their breath...such an animal...so very large and such horns!"

"They looked longer than a man was tall!"

"But the horse and its rider didn't seem to notice at all!"

"They moved as one...and the horse seemed to know the riders intent!"

"Immediately the horse was beside the steer...and the rider was in the air...and again you could see what he was doing..."

"As he came over the top of the steer, he pulled in one leg and his knee came to rest on the far side of the animals horn, and the young man from Montana was reaching as far over as he could to get hold of the animals other horn..."

"And when his weight came down on the horn...the animals head was turned so that he could grab hold and you could see that he was using all his might to pull the animal over..."

"It seemed for a second that the animal would not be brought down...and you knew that everyone was holding their breath...but with the young mans weight and his strength, the animal took a few steps and then you could hear the neck pop!"

"This time the horn the young man was sitting on got stuck in the ground and the steer came over the top and the horn was broken off..."

"The young man was hurt...but even the towns people were cheering!"

"Never had anyone done such a thing!"

"As the young man from Montana was resting from his injury, the steer was being prepared and all the towns people were invited to partake of the celebration."

"That night at the celebration, this song was sung in honor for the young man from Montana...and on the way home, the people kept singing the song and congratulating him and thanking him...and everyone was filled and happy."

"The towns people and the Lakota exchanged gifts and were made friends...and it was the young man from Montana who had done this."

The young boy did not try to make the clouds turn into parts of the story as his grandmother was speaking...he could see in his mind exactly what was happening as if he was there in person.

"What a brave young man he was!"

"And he wasn't even from our people either!" he said to his grandmother.

The boy's father and grandfather had been listening...and they had their eyes closed too, and the young boy knew that they also were seeing the young man from Montana as his grandmother had recounted the story...

But now the work was done and it was time to go home. As they gathered their things together, the young boy started to sing the song.

Lakota hoksila
(Indian boy)

Blachi yiyo!
(Be courageous)

sunka akun wan
(The horse you have to ride)

kokipapelo
(Everyone is afraid of it)

oyuspechola
(with nothing to hold on too)

akun nakinkte
(You must ride him out!)

Hau!

"NO NEWS IS GOOD NEWS!"

From the Author

Sometimes life's experiences leave us feeling drained and feeling hopeless. Dealing with problems others cannot comprehend seems to be a daily part of Lakota life...

In my next offering, we will have a first hand account of a young man's life changing experience with his father and his grandfather...sometime things happen which threaten to change our very lives, including our life's direction and our personal beliefs, and the outside influences which weave our life's patterns...and we change the once thought "unchangeable..."

A gunfight in Vietnam changed my life forever, as well as it took my uncle's life...it should have taken mine also...maybe it has...only I don't know that it has...what I do know is, the hardest thing I've ever had to do in my entire life, was to face my grandfather, and try to explain why I should remain his grandson...and I couldn't defend myself.

My grandfather's sons are all veterans, as are most all his grandchildren and great-grandchildren. So...it was a crushing defeat when he spoke those words to me...it has taken me over thirty years to recover from that crushing blow. But more importantly my grandfather stood by his words and I was never able to get close to him again, only in my thoughts and dreams...and in my prayers.

In 1996 we buried him at Black Hills National cemetery...alone.

But what was most distressing is that he allowed this personal loss of his to consume him entirely and completely. He died with no friends, his relatives had all forsaken him, and only about 12 of us attended his memorial service...

But I have never stopped loving my grandfather, or my father, even when my father didn't say anything in my defence...

I remember, as a child, running headlong into my grandfathers arms and he would catch me under my own small arms and toss me into the air, and say "Johnny Jumpup!!, how is my Johnny Jumpup?", and he would give me the biggest hug.

I know that when we meet again, he will be my grandfather again, and he will have forgiven me, as I have already forgiven him...without forgiveness, there can be no healing and our spirit will die, just as my grandfather had died...a broken spirit.

I hope that through my writings and personal experience, if I can help someone, if even one person or that my experience will help someone to have the courage to change their thoughts, and then their lives...that they in turn will take the time and have the same courage to help others...

And now, my next offering...No News Is Good News...

Hau!

"NO NEWS IS GOOD NEWS"

A Short Story
by
Eya Mani

My legs were shaking now as I stood at attention...

The visitors and mourners had started to arrive, and whenever anyone came within 10 feet of the coffin I was standing guard over...I would move smartly from 'parade rest' to 'attention'...and the pain was getting worse...and I was now sweating freely...again.

I was weak from not eating for the last three days, and I knew my old enemy had returned...Malaria.

When we had touched down in Hawaii a few days earlier...on the plane, I was already having the chills, then a fever, and then the chills...and I had prayed that I be allowed too at least make it home before they hospitalized me...as they surely would.

Now I was home, but I now prayed that I be allowed to make it at least as far as the funeral, which was scheduled for the next morning, but I knew I was much to weak for that to be allowed...and I felt guilty for knowing it.

The man in the coffin was my uncle...the oldest of my father's three younger brothers from my paternal grandfather's second marriage...he was two years younger than I was...and now he was dead.

Five days ago, we had been in a three day gunfight in the Ashau Valley of the Song Thu Bon River in Vietnam...I had been home for two days now, and the shock of being home from one extreme environment to another was overwhelming.

With the extreme environment changes, and my sickness, I was in a daze and delirious, remembering, thinking, dreaming, imagining, and through it all was an enormous guilt that was growing. I found myself wishing I could change places with my uncle, or that I could at least be with him, where ever he was...

I remembered that he and I had hitchhiked to Denver in the summer of 1967, to seek employment...the trip had taken us 7 days...and we had walked many, many miles. But I also remembered that my uncle, who was two years younger than me, had never said a word of regret about coming on this adventure...but instead, he was very optimistic about what we would do in Denver with our first paychecks...

I also remembered that we had met a young man who was employed by the Colorado State Job Service, and with his help we had secured work on a State sponsored Summer Youth Work Program...that young man's name was Floyd Westerman.

Mr. Westerman had also rented an apartment in which we lived, and we agreed to repay him with our very first paychecks...which we did.

I also remembered "the chicken"...and this brought a smile to my lips...

On moving into the apartment, we had no bedding, no furniture, and nothing to eat...

That is...until my older brother looked into the refrigerator and found a block of ice, and inside this block of ice, was a very small chicken...

My older brother had been in Denver for awhile already, and he had moved in with us to cut expenses...

Now, the three of us were standing in front of the refrigerator looking into the freezer compartment trying to figure out how we would 'cook' this bird once he was free of the ice...

My older brother had found an empty 2 lb. coffee can left by the former tenants, and he immediately started pouring hot water on the 'bird' to thaw it out.

Once thawed out and taken from the freezer, the bird's size became apparent...it was a Capon...or so the label said. But since there wasn't enough bird for one of us to eat, we decided to boil it, since it fit so nicely into the 2 lb. coffee tin.

We had also decided that since our uncle was the youngest, he would have the first can of soup and he could also choose one piece off the chicken...

Through the sweat and the tears...I just had to smile...

After we had received our first paychecks and we had paid him back, we had asked Mr. Westerman to take us to a local music store where we could buy some guitars.

After our purchases, Mr. Westerman wanted to hear what kind of music we played...

After listening to us, he had invited us to "sit-in" with him at the Lair Lounge where he had a nightly show... and we had learned 'Gentle on My Mind' by Glenn Campbell...but now the words had real meaning...

*"I dip my cup of soup back from the gurgling crackling cauldron in some train yard...
...my beard a roughening coal pile...and a dirty hat pulled low 'cross my face...
...through cupped hands round the tin can...I pretend to hold you to my breast and find"*

I had staggered and almost fell...but my older brother had grabbed me and helped me to a chair...then he took me to our oldest brothers house.

Then after cleaning and drying out my dress blues...my older brother put on my uniform and went to stand guard at the coffin...in my stead.

My older brother had just returned from Vietnam only a couple of weeks earlier, and he had been discharged from the Marine Corps when he rotated back to the states. But since he didn't have a set of 'dress blues' of his own...I didn't mind that he wore mine.

This was my family...and two of my cousins who were still "in country..." could not be returned to attend their uncle's funeral...damned the Corps anyway...but I loved the Marine Corps.

Since my return two days earlier, I hadn't seen either my father or grandfather...and I dreaded seeing them, but I knew I must...before I went to the hospital.

And so I asked about them...my oldest brother said our grandfather had been at the town bar since he heard of his son's death...and it was there I would have to go to see my grandfather...and my own father.

Arrangements had been made to transport me to the hospital, and from there I would be air-lifted to Rapid City, and from there I would be flown to Denver's Fitzsimmons Army Hospital for treatment of Malaria.

But I had to see my grandfather first...

As I was walking across the street toward the bar, I kept thinking about my departure from home...my journey into combat...my grandfather's smile...the sadness in his eyes... and the sadness in his words, "No news is good news..."

Now I only wished I had come home under other circumstances...I stopped at the door to catch my breath...and gather my courage...then I opened the door and went in...

The two men were seated in the back of the bar...at a booth facing each other...when I walked up to them and stopped...waiting for recognition...but none came...only silence...

...finally...I had to say something...

"Daddy... I'm really sorry...I couldn't bring him home safe..."

Still no movement from either man...then my choking voice...my tears...

"Grandpa...I'm really sorry I couldn't take better care of your boy...any better...I would trade places with him if I could...please forgive me..."

Still no movement...and the silence was deafening...

No movement...no response...but I waited...then I turned to leave when my grandfather finally spoke...

"If you hadn't joined the Marines...my son wouldn't have joined the Marines..."

"He would be alive today..."

"This is all your fault..."

"I never want to hear your name again...I never want to see your face again...you are no longer my grandson..."

I was shocked...

I turned to my father seated across from my grandfather...

"Daddy...we were in a three day gunfight...I had men to take care of too...he was across the river when he got hit...Daddy..."

My father let out a great groan...then he sat silently...never moving...never saying anything in defense of his youngest son...

I turned and walked out...there was nothing left for anyone to say or do...but I had to carry this enormous guilt that had just been put on my shoulders...and try to deal with it... eventually...somehow...

Climbing into the back of the old station wagon...my brothers had made a bed with the back seat down.

As we drove off...I heard my grandfathers voice again..."No news is good news!"...

And I cried...

Hau!

OYUSPECOLA

From the Author

.

Sometimes someone will touch our life...changing it forever in how we perceive ourselves in another persons eyes. Sometimes we see someone set a standard, and we use that standard to measure what others have accomplished, or more often, what we have accomplished...or hope to accomplish.

My son attended a rodeo this year as a spectator...he had gone with his cousin and some friends. When he came home, he never mentioned anything about it. Whether he liked it or not...usually some speak of riders they thought were good or that had impressed him.

I had also gone to a rodeo earlier this year and I was not impressed either. To me the most memorable thing at that rodeo was the 'bullfighters'...and like my brother said, "I think the animals won..."

Perhaps there's a lesson to be learned here. Perhaps the lesson is...we have no more "hero's"...or perhaps no one has done anything impressive enough for the children to emulate...

As an old cowboy, I still remember the best rodeo I've ever attended...right in our front yard...and the cowboy was really a cowgirl...a real cowgirl.

I don't know where the hero in my story has gone...but I know I won't call her a heroine...and I've not heard her name in over 40 years...

.

I only know that she came into our lives, left an indelible impression, and then she was gone, just as quickly as she had come. But I learned how to live because of what she did that morning...and I learned that great deeds have no gender.

And now...my next offering, "Oyuspecola", meaning...with nothing to hold on too...

Hau!

OYUSPECOLA
(With nothing to hold on to...)

A Short Story
by
Eya Mani

Her name was Barbara...

They said she had been raised by the staff at Pierre Indian School, since she was old enough to go to school.

Now she was in high school, and she had come home for the first time. She had made friends with my sister... then she moved in.

Barbara was not shy, or afraid of anything...if she was, she never let it show...

I think we all liked her because she was more like one of the guys. Although she was a real good cook, she was also one helluva shortstop, and she chopped wood and did what we boys could do, only she did everything better.

I think I remember her best because she could ride, and none of our horses were afraid of her...I know it was her spirit. She was firm and confident... but she was gentle.

We had just moved across the river from Rock Creek that first year, about three miles from town. And in the spring when the river flooded, we had to swim the horses across the river to get to town, and swim them back home.

We usually did this three or four times a day, but we were never afraid. My dad and grandfather showed us how to swim horses, and when the waters were deep and swift, flowing bank to bank with ice bergs floating past...there was no time for dress rehearsal.

So, all in all, Barbara was pretty fearless.

Barbara was also very pretty, but she never paid any attention to her looks...she was just one of the guys...of which we were many.

My grandparents, and my father, took in children, mostly boys, who had no place to go or no one to care for them. They would take in these children and we always had lotsa company...everyone was treated like one of the family.

One morning after breakfast and the morning readings, we all went out to get the horses ready for a ride out to grandma's, about 13 miles out. It was very early, perhaps around 0600 or so, and the air was crisp and cool.
The horses had come home the night before and they were standing around the huge

oak tree just below the house, all except for April, my dad's yearling filly. She was playful that morning. She was going around taking playful nips at the other horses flanks, causing them to mock anger and lay their ears back. Then she would move on to the next horse, until she had them all in a playful mood.

We caught the horses we were going to ride, all except for Barbara, she went up to April and started petting her. April had never been ridden, but she was used to people...when she was six months old, we started putting a halter on her to lead, and finally we put a child's saddle on her back to get her used to carrying weight. She was now a yearling, so all someone had to do was top her off...but this morning she wasn't encumbered with a halter or saddle.

Barbara had been petting April's flanks and now she was rubbing down her legs as we saddled our horses for the long ride out to grandma's. Without any warning, Barbara grabbed April's mane and threw her leg over, mounting up bareback, and in one motion she grabbed the mane and tail...and with a twist of her hands, she got the "bull riders grip"...and we were in for the ride of a lifetime.

April gave her just a second to seat herself, then she was gone...lunging forward in great leaps, one...two...three, scattering and spooking the other horses. We had to recatch our horses and mount up.

Mean while April, with her head swinging from side to side, was trying to fake-out the rider...then she was sunfishing, but Barbara wasn't impressed...she moved with the animal.

April turned North on the road in front of the big house, then they stretched out full gallop following the road going around the hill. By this time we were in hot pursuit, but we could see Barbara and April easily pulling away.

Barbara was leaning forward, prone on the horse's back. She had released the horse's tail and she seemed to be talking to her, petting and rubbing her neck, but the ride continued and we were left behind as they raced on out of sight.

Around the bend was a stand of trees where there was a bend in the road, here Barbara and April raced past us going back in the direction of home. We all slammed on the brakes and turned our horses around and followed.

When the house came into view, Barbara and April were at the hitching post.

Barbara was still on April's back but she was leaning forward petting the horses neck and she was talking to her...April would paw the ground and neigh softly.

Dad was standing outside the loghouse laughing...belly laughing. He made a few comments about Paul Revere's ride...someone else mentioned Icabod Crane and the Headless Horseman...we all had a good laugh but I know us boys felt sheepish, maybe a little ashamed for not taking the initiative to do what Barbara had done.

Barbara rode April out to grandma's that day. No saddle, no bridle, no halter. If she wanted to turn she would gently slap April's neck and April would turn in the opposite direction...if she wanted to stop she would pull on her mane...and to break her into a run, she would gently nudge her in the ribs.

Its been 40 years since that early morning ride. Inside the space of 15 minutes we had a real S _ _ t kicker of a rodeo, a wild horse ride, and a lesson in horsemanship that has lasted me a lifetime.

"Horse Whisperer", eat your heart out!!!

Hau!

(For Barbara)

PURGATORY

From the Author

In March 1998 I returned from the VA Hospital in Hot Springs, SD. The very first thing I heard was that the young men and women of Standing Rock Reservation were killing themselves...

The Tribal Council was unable to deal with this...

They brought in a few 'experts' and called a few meetings and let it go at that, but the suicides continued and no one would actively do anything about it.

Even the parents were turned away when they went to look for help...

Every agency and department of the tribe, the Bureau of Indian Affairs, and the Indian Health Service thought the parents of these unfortunate children were asking for "MONEY"... when they asked them for help, and all were turned away.

When in fact, all the parents were asking for was family counseling, one on one, or perhaps a safe house for the remaining siblings...and money was never mentioned in any case, at least not by the parents of any of the victims.

1997 and 1998 has been a very trying time on Standing Rock, and only time will tell if the people will get a workable tribal council in place, and if they will heal properly by taking care of themselves as they have done so many times in the past.

The people have even approached the Inspector Generals Office, the Federal Bureau of Investigation, and we even went to see a Federal Judge, with no satisfaction. It can only be expected that the practices of the tribal council will continue until such time as the people have had enough.

In January 2000, my own daughter tried suicide. Not one counselor, social service worker, councilman, police officer, child protection team member, or anyone else ever visited my home.

It is my hope and sincere expectation that something positive will happen very soon...

My next offering, Purgatory, is a cynical but truthful look at the Standing Rock Tribal Government and the establishment...

Hau!

PURGATORY
(a temporary place of punishment, expiation, or remorse)

A
Poem
by
Eya Mani

And the preacher said,
"Its against God's law to take your own life, if you do you go straight to hell!"
But when they laid him to rest, the preacher said,
"Today this young man is with the Lord...in a better place!"
So 12 more kids went to look for rope...

The Board of Directors said,
"This is the 'Lodge of Good Voices', come and have your own Radio Program!"
But when Tribal members got together they were told,
"You cannot talk about sexual harrassment, job discrimination, or nepotism!"
So 12 more kids went to look for rope...

When the Tribal members said,
"You have taken all our powers for yourself, to hire, to spend, to develop... why?"
The Tribal Council members looked the other way and said,
"Because we can!"
So 12 more kids went to look for rope...

The Tribal Judge said,
"If you don't like what they are doing, there is an Election coming up!"
So the People voted out the Tribal Judge...and replaced some Councilmen,
but the new Tribal Council hired the deposed Judge as Legal Counsel...
So 12 more kids went to look for rope...

And the snow came, and the flood followed,
and 22 families lost their homes...so FEMA gave the Tribe $4.29 Million
but the People had to pay for their own snow removal anyway...
because the Tribal Council went on Vacation...to Las Vegas
So 12 more kids went to look for rope...

The People went to the I.G. and the F.B.I...and a Federal Judge
and they brought their evidence and their testimony
All the I.G. and the F.B.I. would say was,
"We're sorry, but the Tribal Council didn't take enough!"
So 12 more kids went to look for rope...

Now I sit and wonder...about the rightness of it all
and is there really Justice?...when will our Tribal Council take a fall?
My mind keeps going back...'cause surely there is a God?
and I wonder if the Tribal Council ever thinks or dreams...
What would happen... when the kids stop looking for rope?

Hau!

REACHOUT, AND TOUCH SOMEONE...

From the Author

My grandmother once said that being Lakota was much more than being different from anyone else...to be Lakota was to be aware.

One had to think all the time...about what they were doing, things they had to do and how to do them properly, how to act and treat others, but most importantly, it was a way of life...one had to pray in everything they did...

From the time of my earliest remembrances, until I lost both my grandparents in the mid 1980's, my time away from them was only a few years.

On my many journeys, when I returned home they were the first ones I would go and see. As they got older, I could feel their spirits growing stronger, and I wanted so, to be like them.

They knew things...I don't know how they knew, but they knew things...and I think it was their spirit.

Another quality I've observed in them, and one which I have not seen since, that was the ability to be discussing something important, then stop abruptly and discuss something else...then to come back days, weeks, or months later and continue that same conversation they had so abruptly left off earlier.

One day my brother and I were hunting and we shot a young doe. It was a mistake, but she was dead. Knowing that grandma would be angry with us for being so thoughtless, we cut off the head, the feet and the flanks, then we skinned it out. When we brought home the deer, my grandmother just sat and looked at it quietly. After a time she told grandpa to hitch up the team. Then she asked where had we killed this young mother and she had us show them. Then we had to scour the brush and find the day old fawn, which we brought home and raised...

How did she know...?

One summer it was time to can the wild fruit, so we went and picked what grandma needed. Everyone knew what to do so we all worked in silence. Then grandpa went to town and got the jars, lids, sugar, and jell.

On the first day, grandma sorted the fruit and boiled them, while grandpa boiled the jars and lids. When he had finished, he asked if that was enough, and grandma said, "yes", so grandpa filled the jars and put the lids on loose.

The second day, grandpa tightened all the lids and grandma inspected and labeled them.

All that was said was, "Is this good...?" and grandma's reply..."yes..."

The third day grandma sorted them all out and packed them away. Then we loaded them into the wagon and we went around and gave everyone fresh jam and syrup. After we finished grandpa asked, "Did we get everyone...?" and again grandma's reply, "yes", so we went back home.

That was the quietest three days I had ever spent with my grandparents, but I will always remember it...my next offering, "Reachout and Touch Someone..."

Hau!

REACH OUT AND TOUCH SOMEONE...

A Short Story
by
Eya Mani

...the naked man had a rope tied around his neck and he was being led around by the children and women. When he tried to cover his nakedness the leather rope was jerked and he came to his knees, he was beaten with sticks and stones were thrown at him. All the while the women and children laughed and pointed fingers at him...

The old lady had had enough, and she finally jumped to her feet and shouted in her native tongue, "Who said we lived like that...who said we treated others like that...who said we allow our children to behave like this...?" Then she stormed out the door with the other elders, mostly women, following closely behind her... muttering words of anger and disgust as they exited the building.

The young man's grandfather said, "Johnny, can you take grandma home? I want to stay and see what happens..."

On the trip home his grandmother sat in angered silence, staring out the pickup window into the black night.

The young man tried to apologize to his grandmother, but she silenced him with "Quiet, tomorrow we will talk of these things..."

As he helped his grandmother from the truck, she said, "Tuweni asabmaya wacinsni..." or, "I do not want anyone to make me dirty..." then she went into the house and slammed the door.

The movie they had been watching was the opening scenes of "A Man Called Horse..."

On the trip home his grandfather exclaimed, "Whoever heard? Did you see that? I wonder why they made it like that? We were never like that...but of course, you can never tell anyone that. If they knew how we really are, they wouldn't make any movies about us..." then he chuckled and said, "Ohhh jimminy..."

The next morning, all his grandmother said about the night before was, "Today... don't touch anyone..."

The young man asked his father about that statement, and all his father said was, "Listen, and you will understand..."

That weekend he was visiting with his other grandfathers. One lived in Rapid City and one lived in here in McIntosh.

The two old timers were visiting in their language, and the young man sat listening and laughing with them, because they liked to tell funny stories and joke a lot.

Just before the noon meal, a car drove in and parked in the driveway, and a young woman got out.

She knocked and came in, and after greeting everyone, she had dinner.

After dinner, she sat silent in a chair she had set in the corner of the room.

Without being told, the young man said he had some things to do, then he left, returning only when the car was gone.

The young man was about to ask the question, when his grandfathers spoke...

"So...did she put the touch on you...?" one grandfather asked the other...

"Yes...she said she wanted to move back home now, and needed some help..."

"Well...she put the touch on me too...so she must have enough to do her business..."

It was a few years later that his grandmother asked him.

"What did you learn about being touched by another...?"

The youngman thought about this before answering...

"You don't have to be touched physically by another...if children would keep their hands too themselves there wouldn't be any trouble, but that's only one way to touch someone."

"People can touch another by spreading rumor and gossip...they can touch another by slashing their car tires..."

"They can also touch an entire family by not giving someone a job...and in some cases, an entire village can be touched by what the leaders do...or what they don't do..."

"But touching someone isn't all bad either..."

"You can help someone, give someone a job...or help them in some way...so I must watch what I do when I am around another who needs help, sometimes I think I am helping...when really I am not..."

"Okay..." his grandmother said with quiet approval...then she continued.

"If you have to do something, or if you have to make a decision...if there is any doubt in your heart, then don't do it, because it is probably wrong..."

"But if there is no doubt and your heart tells you that it is the right thing to do...then do it, and without asking anything in return..."

As the young man went to help his grandfather stake out the horses, his grandfather said, "You know...grandma told all her kids the same things she tells you. I think only your dad listened...but sometimes I don't know either...now she is telling you guys the same things, and we are waiting to see who is listening...that was quite a movie ennit..."

... then he chuckled again...and started home.

Hau!

SAVING GEORGIA

From the Author

When I was a young man and I wanted to get married, my grandmother took me aside and said, "What you want is good, but you must know one thing. After you marry and have children, you will no longer have a life of your own. You must take care of your children, they come first in your life, all decisions must be made in consideration of your children."

Sometimes being a parent is very trying, but my grandmother also let me know one of her secrets..."One of the things you must do everyday is to pray for your children's safety, and you must also help those less fortunate...this will ensure that your children will be safe..."

In the summer of 1999 I took a group of Elders to LaFramboise Island in Pierre, SD for a meeting. I asked three elders about 'child rearing' and they all had the same answer although each was from a different band of the Lakota Nation.

I found this very interesting...

My question was: "What am I doing wrong in raising my kids? I provide for them well, my wife and I don't gamble or run around drinking, we don't use dope, and we raised our children to pray and to know the Creator, the culture, and to respect people. So what am I doing wrong?"

At this particular time it seemed that at any given time three of our six children were into some kind of trouble and we didn't know what to do...

One elder Yanktonai gentleman said, "You are not doing anything wrong. Everyone must experience life. How will they know good if they do not experience bad, or know cold if they do not touch the fire and know heat? Don't worry about your children, they have to experience these things, that is life, if you have raised them well they will experience the bad and they will let it go. Just continue the way you have been taught and they will be alright..."

An elderly lady from my community said the same thing, as did another elderly gentleman from the Pine Ridge Reservation.

Wisdom is sometimes so simple and obvious, but in our anxiety and confusion as parents, we tend to forget, as I had.

We have since returned to a more "normal" life again and all my children are doing well...sometimes there is a slip but we recover and go on with our lives.

With this, I wish all parents well and their children also...there is much wisdom in our elders... we must never forget to ask them.

And now...a tribute to our young people, and my beautiful daughter...

Hau!
(for Georgia True Love)

SAVING GEORGIA

A Poem
by
Eya Mani

A baby girl...Native American...A China doll
with laughing eyes like no other!
She made me think about it when she was four
she walked up to the Doctor and said
"If you make me cry my Daddy will be mad at you!"

We took her to Oklahoma...then to Kansas City
she just started school and everybody loved her!
She made us laugh in Aberdeen
when she turned to her Mom and said
"When I'm sick chocolate makes me feel better!"

She was in High School...and I made tipi's
she made her own clothes...and Mom waited up late for her
but we were proud when she graduated in '94
then went on to finish Job Corps in the Black Hills and she said
"Thank you for believing in me...I love you Mom and Dad"

Our China doll goes to College at United Tribes
she has a personality like no other
she works part time and we can't keep up!
her sister called the other day and said
"she's sitting here with two black eyes!"

When her Mom asked what happened?
she corrected herself and said
"No, I mean she's sitting here with two Black guys!!!"
I give thanks for her everyday and pray
because deep down I know she's really saving Dad...

Hau!

SMARTGIRL

From the Author

Smartgirl came about by my wanting to get a business partner for my tipi company, which had been defunct for the last three years. I had placed an ad on the Internet and this lady had responded...and we founded a new friendship.

Our friendship lasted only a short time, perhaps three weeks at most, and I was not eager to end our relationship...but I knew I had too.

Being Lakota, I am keenly aware of people and where their interests lie, and what, if any, their motives might be, or whether they are sincere in their endeavors.

I felt I was not being treated truthfully by my new friend...and what other societies and cultures see as normal and acceptable...are not acceptable in the Lakota Culture.

Honesty, wholesomeness, and total commitment to a planned event are some of the things we treasure as we struggle to achieve whatever perfection we feel we need for success. Using someone to achieve our ends is not Lakota culture, especially anything for personal gain... and so our friendship ends...just as abruptly as it began...

Almost fitting I would think...but this poem won me the right to go to Reno, Nevada in 1999 and return Poet Laureate...

...and now...I call my next offering...Smartgirl.

Hau!

SMARTGIRL

A Poem
by
Eya Mani

She said, "I meet all the qualifications...now what?"
I said, "Its good to meet you...I quit smoking today."
She said, "Tell me about yourself and your family..."
So I did, and I introduced her to my cousin Gill...

She said, "Can you come and talk to the kids at my school?"
I said, "I just need expenses and I will be there."
She said, "You really gave a good talk, can you come here again?"
So we made plans, and we talked about my cousin Gill...

She said, "Do you think I'm pretty? Tell me what you really think."
I said, "Yes, you are very pretty...you are unapproachable."
She said, "My boyfriend Jack doesn't think so..."
So we talked about her boyfriend Jack, and my cousin Gill...

She said, "Jack and I are planning to buy property...to share."
So I asked, "Why then are you looking for a husband?"
She said, "Just in case Jack and I end up alone, we will have each other,
and the property...we'll share..."
So I thought about her boyfriend Jack, and my cousin Gill...

I said, "I cannot be your friend, if you do not know what you have just said, and if you do
not know what you have said, then I cannot explain it..."

Hau!

SOUP AND FRYBREAD

From the Author

Many of my stories originate at a place known as Pine-Little Eagle, now just a church and a cemetery.

But this was once part of the King Ranch...an outfit from Texas who came up north and leased thousands of acres of Indian lands, because it was cheap...but it is where I was raised as a child...it was family land.

Although the family still owns the land, The Bureau of Indian Affairs has managed to divide the family, by dividing its holdings...

Straight Pine, patriarch of the Pine Tiospaye, was a nephew of our great leader Sitting Bull. And his cousin Little Eagle, patriarch of the Little Eagle Tiospaye, settled here with their families after July 1873, when Standing Rock was designated a reservation.

Sitting Bull, while working in Wild Bill's traveling Wild West show, was once asked for his address of residence. He gave it simply as Grand River...this is the area he was referring to.

Although many of the deeds accomplished by my 'modern' relatives are not as well known as those of the great warriors, they have still accomplished many things that even today are not practiced, by any standards.

The men and women of my childhood, somehow seemed more mature, more intelligent, and more dynamic than today's person. That is what I wish to share with you in these stories of my childhood.

It is my hope that through my sharing these stories of personal sacrifice and quiet simplicity, I can somehow help to bring back those values we all once shared...

And now...I offer..."Soup and Frybread..."

Hau!

"SOUP AND FRYBREAD"

*A Short Story
by
Eya Mani*

I cut the motor on the Yardman lawnmower...then I sat down on the end gate of the pickup truck, which I had parked by the cemetery entrance...

After the noise in my ears had cleared, I could hear Anne Murray's "Can I Have This Dance...(For the rest of my life)" playing on the radio. One of the kids was listening to the radio and it seemed fitting that this song would be on now...

It had been my father's favorite song...

I had been cutting the grass in the cemetery for almost two hours now, and I was finally finished.

My wife had been pulling weeds and cleaning the graves for that time also, and we now stopped for a picnic lunch we had brought...

The boys had been at the river...they had taken their air rifles and fishing poles, but they didn't come to catch fish. They would bring these items to pass the time and to explore the draws and creeks, much the same as I had done as a child.

But now we were hungry...

After lunch I returned to the graves and started cleaning them one by one, starting with my fathers grave. As always, I would think about the life and my association with the person who's grave I was cleaning.

Now I said a prayer...and as I worked, I let myself go back in time...long ago.

The sacrifices this man had made, so I could be warm and dressed well enough to not be self conscious, while going to an unfamiliar school.

That year, winter came early, and my father had taken a job as a ranch hand in a town some...100 miles away.

One evening, just when the heating fuel and the food ran out, this man had come home.

He was cold and shivering...he wasn't dressed for the cold, and although I could see his obvious misery, he was happy to be home.

I remembered that he had let me stay home from school the next day so we could go down to Elfrink's, and buy that pair of cowboy boots I had been admiring for sometime.

It was only later that I had learned of my father's wish, to buy that old car that the Heinrich's had been saving for him. He had said nothing, but had let us kids buy what ever we had wanted...and the next day, he hitchhiked back to work.

I was finished, so I got to my feet, and I apologized... "I'm so sorry Daddy, I didn't know..."

As I moved over to my grandfather's grave, a faint smile came to my lips...

I always remembered my grandfather as someone who made interesting things happen.

Kneeling, I started to pull the thorns my wife had left behind...long, long ago...

We had been hunting the very elusive pronghorn antelope all day...and I was getting very tired...

My grandfather was in a wagon, pulled by a team of two very large Belgian horses, while I had been trying to sneak up on these antelope for most of the day...he was trying to maneuver himself around to get the antelope to come toward me...it didn't work.

These antelope seemed to read my thoughts, and when I would try to cut in front of them, they would change course, and I would end up miles away, and I would have to start over...but I just had to smile.

My grandfather had been a cook in the US Army during WWII...but that did not show his ability to shoot with his rifle...he was an excellent shot with his 7 mm.

The antelope won. I quit...I was heading back toward the wagon which grandpa had parked on a hill, about a mile away.

I was in deep thought...hot, tired, hungry, and not a little angry at myself for not being "sneaky enough" to outwit these stupid animals...

I seldom went home empty handed, but I was...and I found myself making excuses why I didn't like antelope meat...

It was too light, like veal, it didn't have the protein (as if I knew that for sure), they weren't as tasty as their larger eared cousins, who always stopped at the top of the hill for one last look...which was their last look...!

As I stumbled along, not really watching where I was going...I heard the shot.

The report of my grandfather's rifle, was followed by the sound of the bullet traveling across the prairie, followed by a loud "thud"...

I ran up the nearest hilltop to see where the stricken antelope was...

As we loaded the antelope into the wagon, my grandfather was surprised that no visible signs of gunshot could be found...there was no blood, but the animal was not breathing either, so he must be dead...?

As we winded our way home on the many wagon trails that crossed our path, the animal lifted its head and looked at us dizzily...

My grandfather gave a shout, and we got down and immediately tied up the pronghorn buck with the rope my grandfather always carried.

When we got within sight of the log house, the animal started to make sounds like a sheep, but more guttural. This continued until we pulled into the yard of the house, and then everyone came running to see what the noise was...

After hearing the story of the hunt, and after seeing the awakened buck antelope, no one wanted to carry out the execution, for that's what it would have been. Everyone had a good laugh and on close examination of the antelope, my grandfather found a very small knick in one of the antelope's pronged horns.

"Miss you grandfather..." I whispered as I moved on to uncle Elmer's grave...

1959...It was a very bad year...no rain and none forecast.

The cattlemen and ranchers had to sell their livestock at very low prices. The Rivers and Creeks dried up. Everything and everyone took a beating that year, and dust was every where...

But I remembered 1959 as uncle Elmer's year...one of the best years I could remember as a kid...

I had noticed my uncle pace back and forth daily, talking in hushed whispers with his brother.

This continued for about a week, then one day, they were both gone...

They hadn't spoken to anyone, so no one knew what they had discussed, or where they had gone.

The months came and went, and the family did what they could to survive, and still no one heard from either uncle. Grandma was starting to get worried...this was not like her boys...surely something bad had happened to them!

School had started, and Halloween and Thanksgiving came and went, and still no sign or word from either uncle. Now I was getting worried...Christmas was coming soon and my grandmother was preparing something special for her two absent boys...

Everyone knew something was about to happen, only what...?

On Christmas Eve, late in the evening, a pickup truck drove into the yard and my two uncles got out.

I could hear them laughing and talking with the driver...then everyone was outside hugging and greeting each other. I was so glad to see them...and grandma's prayers had been answered...but that wasn't all!

The uncles had been out working all summer and fall...and they had brought presents for everyone in the family, the kids got two each, and food...!

No one was left out...grandma even took some to the neighbors, and everyone had a truly good Christmas...in 1959.

I remembered.

I just cried and cried...I couldn't stop, so I went out into the cold and cried by myself...I was so glad to see that my uncles were alright...

Yes, it was uncle Elmer's year. If I ever had a hero, it was my uncle Elmer.

"Thank you uncle..." I whispered as I got up to leave...

I was getting fatigued now...I have arthritis in my back, and my wife knew of my pain and discomfort, so she said, "I think we better be getting home now, the chiggers and the mosquitoes will be out soon, and I don't want to put up with that..."

While the boys loaded up the lawn mower and tools, I closed the cemetery gate and I said to my wife..."I know what we can have for supper when we get home...soup and fry bread!"

Hau!

TOKA WASTE KTE

From the Author

There has been much talk of the Lakota losing their culture...this should not be allowed to happen.

Many of the "Old Ones" are leaving us now and it is up to us to make sure this does not happen. One way to keep the culture alive is to continue the storytelling, and keep it as accurate as we can so as not to bastardize our culture...this is my greatest fear.

As in the story, 'Grandma knew everything, but you had to ask', that is the way of the old ones. They seldom offered anything, you had to want to learn, you had to ask why. That is the reality of youth. You can ask why without being validated, without fear of reprisal, and if you ask the right person, you will have the correct answer and the reasons for it being the right answer.

There are many ways to get a name, but one never, never names themselves like they do today. The names came from the People, and in keeping with the tradition that the name be earned...for whatever reason.

In our story the renaming of the Lakota Warrior came at midlife, when the earning of names usually took place when the men were still young, but his deeds and the compassion he offered the enemy at a most crucial time in his life, tells of the true character of the man.

In the telling of Lakota stories we do not dwell on the inner battles of conscience or personal anguish, but rather we will tell of these only to let the reader know that there is a real conflict of cultures as in the story of "The Deer Hunter".

And now, "TOKA WASTE KTE"....

Hau!

TOKA WASTE KTE

A Short Story

by

Eya Mani

The two boys had spent the morning chopping wood for the old man who lived behind their grandmothers log house. Then they went from log house to log house and hauled water in buckets from the well in the middle of the community.

No one told them to do it...tt was something they did willingly and it was enough when the old ones looked at them with approving eyes and a hint of a smile.

Now it was almost noon and they sat on the big hill behind the Episcopal Church and looked down on the town. It wasn't much to see really. A store with a post office, a Catholic Church on the east hill, the Congregational Church which stood in the west part of town just east of their grandmothers, and the BIA School which went to the 6th grade.

The younger of the two boys started naming all the people they had helped that morning. Bears Rib, Sees the Bear, Grey Eagle, Knocks Him Down, Eagle Pipe, Cedar Boy, and their aunt who was married to a man named Kills Pretty Enemy.

Their naming of the people turned to "how do you think they got their names...?"

Neither of them knew although the older boy made up stories of gallantry in battle and brave deeds and the younger boy settled on that.

But he was intrigued...how did the old ones get their names?

He would ask grandma...grandma knew everything but you had to ask.

The two boys raced down the hill and as usual, the older boy let the younger boy win and the younger boy would mock protest although he too knew that it was a gesture, being the older boys little brother...he felt good about his big brother.

They ate breakfast in silence and when they were finished eating, they made sure the wood was cut and the water buckets were full. Their grandmother had gone outside to start making pa-pa from the mule deer buck hanging from the shade. The older boy had gone to play with the older boys, but the younger boy was always close by grandma.

He would help her hang up the meat to dry after she had cut it into thin slices.

Preparing...always preparing for the unseen events which would be forth coming...

Finally the boy couldn't hold his question any longer... "Grandma, who named all these people? I mean, how did they get their names...?"

No answer...his grandmother continued to hum the song she always hummed when she was content with her work...

He was going to ask her again when she looked at him and smiled...

"Grandson, where does that come from...?"

"Do you really want to know...?"

"Come sit here and sharpen these knives for me...and when you are finished I will tell you..."

When the boy had finished sharpening the knives his grandmother came out of the log house and they ate lunch...

When they had finished eating...she asked him, "Who do you want to know about...?"

The boy was puzzled because he had never really thought about it, but he said "uncle Gilbert..."

"How did he get his name?"

"That one..." his grandmother said matter of factly...her voice trailing off...the boy could see she was in deep thought as she continued...

"It is a story of great pain... and great love..."

His grandmother turned to look into his eyes to make sure he understood what she was about to tell him...

"But you cannot have one...without the other..."

The young boy settled down and got comfortable...when his grandmother told him stories of "long ago," he would close his eyes and he could see the story unfold before him...like those "moving pictures" the older kids got to go watch at the school every summer...only he didn't have to go anywhere...he had grandma.

When he was comfortable...the story began...

"Your uncle got his name from his father...but it was one of his fathers that got that name from the People...or so it is said..."

"It all happened long ago...before the coming of the whites..."

"It is said that among the young warriors...there was a man who was very well known and respected among the People...he did everything he could for them, more than was expected of him, and all the fathers wanted him to choose one of their daughters to be his woman..."

"But...the young man continued...and he made a name for himself among the People..."

"One day...he did choose a young woman to be his...but by now he was not so young...but nevertheless, he remained a great warrior among the people and his name was spread far among the other bands of the Lakota..."

"It is said that one day when all the men were out of camp, the Crow had come and had stolen some horses and they had also taken some women...and they took them back into Crow country...which is far away..."

"One of the women that they had taken was this warriors woman..."

"It is said that he left immediately to hunt down the Crow..."

"He didn't wait for anyone to go with him...he went alone..."

"It is said that he rode right into the Crow camp and went boldly from lodge to lodge but that he couldn't find the woman...and after many days he returned to the People, who all thought her dead now, because some time had passed..."

"This great Lakota warrior was alone now...for most of the time, and the people knew that he must be in great pain...because he really cared for that woman..."

"One day it was heard that a Lakota woman was living with the Crow at such and such a place..."

"When this warrior heard that, he left immediately...alone...and he rode into the Crow camp and stole that woman back..."

"It is said that he rode into the camp with such fury that the Crow ran away...thinking that the Lakota surely had come to kill the entire camp...they didn't know that it was only one man..."

"It is said that the woman he brought back...was not the same woman that was taken some years back..."

"It is also said that when the Crow came after the woman again...that she went back willingly...and that she even ran away to be with this Crow..."

"It is said...that she had two children from this Crow...and that was why she had run away..."

"This time the Lakota warrior did not follow...but he thought a very long time about this..."

"But he had to do what he had to do...and so, one day he put on his finest dress...and he took his finest horses...and he went back again to the Crow camp..."

"But this time he rode in close...and he asked the woman to return to him...and to bring her children with her...and all would be well..."

"If she came with him...and if she brought her children...then he would let the Crow live, and they would leave in peace..."

"But the woman would not go, and the Crow, thinking that this one Lakota warrior who surely was dressed to die, would be an easy kill..."

"And so the Crow mocked him...and made fun of him...and they taunted him...but the Lakota warrior seemed to pay them no mind..."

"It is said that the Lakota warrior asked her a second time...to bring the children and return with him to their own people...but she would not...and that she had also mocked him...and taunted him...and laughed at him..."

"It is said that even the horses, when they heard what the Crow and the woman had said, they also knew what they had to do...they too were getting furious, and they were stomping their feet and prancing around, eager for the fight..."

"It is said that the Lakota warrior rode in with such fury that the Crow became confused and afraid, and they started to run everywhere...trying to escape..."

"It is said that all the Crow warriors were killed quickly...and with such a vengeance that only the woman, her two children, and the Crow who had stolen her were left alive..."

"And again...the third time...the Lakota warrior asked her to come with him, and to bring her children, and he would let the Crow live..."

"But in her anger...and in her fear...she would not..."

"And so, it is said that the Lakota warrior told her that if that was her choice, then she would be with the Crow forever…and he killed them both…"

"The People say…that he brought those two children back to live with him among his own People…and he raised them as Lakota warriors, and that they also were very fine men…"

"And from that time, the People called him, 'Kills Pretty Enemy'…because his woman was very fair and good to look upon…but that she had chosen the Crow over him…and he had to do what he had to do…"

With that, the story was finished…his grandmother sat a few moments deep in thought…then she got up and went back into the log house.

The young boy sat in awed silence…replaying the scenes over and over again in his mind…

Then he got his bow and arrows and went to play with his friends, never saying a word of this to anyone…it was his secret…but maybe he would share this with his brother…someday.

Hau!

TUWA OYAKE NA

From the Author

"Someone Said" is a journey of the Lakota Veteran, from his birth to his return home from war, and on into the middle years of his life.

The Lakota Veteran is "unfortunate" because the people have forgotten how to depend on him and his abilities as a protector and a provider. Instead he is looked down on as a drunk, uneducated, unskilled, unclean, and unwanted.

While the above is now true to some degree, it was not always so...

The Lakota Veteran learned at a very young age to be disciplined, responsible, courageous, and compassionate.

Because the Lakota of today choose to take the white man's education over the traditional Lakota culture, all the old customs and traditions are thrown aside and they are replaced by the work ethic, personal greed, the acquiring of personal goods at any cost, and selfishness...thus causing confusion in both the home and in our tribal government.

Tuwa Oyake Na is written in the way the "old ones" would speak. Every sentence begins with "Tuwa Oyake Na" and can be translated "Someone Said" or "It has been heard" or even... "It is reported."

This poem illustrates how the People are being assimilated into the role of the "forgotten" and the "oppressed", much as the Lakota Veterans are. Only by standing up for themselves, can they overcome the poverty and the condition they have become accustomed too, and take the authority back from the leadership and regain all that was lost.

This work took over two years to write...the words are those of the elders, the veterans and others whom I've spoken with about what we've lost as a People...

Its become a memorial to my cousin Percy Little Eagle...and my beloved uncle Chauncey Long Elk...I'll miss you both...you've taught me so many things...

And now..."Someone Said"...

Hau!

TUWA OYAKE NA
(Someone said)

A Poem
by
Eya Mani

Someone said,
When he was born, the grandmothers cried, the grandmothers cried
because he would be different, he would be blessed, but he would have a very hard time,
Someone said,

Someone said,
Today! It rained on him today and on no one else! He is different I know!
He who is blessed, but he will have a very hard time
Someone said,

Someone said,
He is raised in the old way, he has learned to ride in the wind and the rain and when the
horse's ears spark blue, he has learned the wisdom of his grandmother, and he
keeps the knowledge of his grandfather, he is blessed, but he will have a very hard time,
Someone said,

Someone said,
Where is he? He who is blessed? He is on his travels, he follows the path of his
fathers. He is learning a great many things but he will return again. He who is blessed,
but he will have a very hard time,
Someone said,

Someone said,
There is a battle raging and he has gone to fight! He is with the children of his brother,
and with the brother of his father, but he will return again unharmed, he who is
blessed, and then he will have a very hard time,
Someone said,

Someone said,
Where is he? He who was blessed? There is no one left to lead! And those who would
have chosen the path of the white metal. There is a great hunger and the
old ones perish! And our young ones choose to leave with the old! And now we have
a very hard time!
Someone said,

Someone said,
All is silent. There is no one to speak for the people
The men are silent and the women are angry, and the children have no one
to care or to feed them, and we have a very hard time
Someone said,

Someone said,
But where is he? He who was blessed? He who is learned in the old ways?

And Someone said,
He has returned and no one knew it! He has returned and no one has welcomed
him back among the people! He has returned but is forgotten, we have
had a very hard time,
Someone said,

Someone said,
We must go and speak with him, and we must bring him back into the circle,
and we must learn the ways of the old ones.
Someone said,

Someone said,
He is returned and he is sick and cannot lead, and he cannot serve the people!
He has no place and he is cold and hungry, and he has a very hard time,
Someone said,

And Someone said,
If you would honor him, then you must ask him. If you would feed him, you must invite
him. If you would have him lead, then you must follow, and if you would learn, you
must ask him to teach,
Someone said,

And Someone said,
Let us go now and ask him, that he may come once again to his people,
let us ask him and invite him, and follow him, and learn from him. and it may be
that he will come again, to live among the people, and ease the burden of the People,
Someone said.

Hau!

WANAGI
(Ghost)

From the Author

The Lakota call Alcohol "Mni Wakan" or "Spirit Water".

My grandparents used to say it made the people who drank it act crazy...

Early on during my childhood, alcohol use was looked down on by the People, and anyone who used alcohol was ostracized, ignored, or sometimes very openly humiliated...depending on who the offended party was.

Because the People rejected the use of alcohol, some persons who imbibed were forced to use alcohol in secret. And because the sale of alcohol to Indians was illegal until around 1953 those who used it were forced to find other means to get "drunk".

In their search for alcohol some users even drained their automobile radiators, or bought automobile "antifreeze", thinking this was the same type of alcohol sold in bars and liquor stores, but it is not.

Drinking of this "wood alcohol" was very dangerous. Its side effects included blindness and temporary blindness, loss of body functions, paralysis, insanity, and even death.

To help deter the younger people from using alcohol in any manner, the old ones told stories about the "Evil Spirits" which came alive when people used alcohol, or do bad things to others...

Wanagi is such a story...and my next offering.

Wanagi is meant to be a writing of "Creative Non-fiction"...what do you think?

Hau!

WANAGI
(Evil Spirit)

A Short story
by
Eya Mani

The man stood overlooking the view. It was beautiful. At first he didn't seem to see the activity below. First the dog, taken by surprise, let out a sharp bark, then recognizing the visitor, bounded up the hill, tail waving frantically.

The visitor went back to the pickup truck and grabbed the cold beer he knew would be welcome. He stopped again to take in the view, noticing the channel had changed in the White Shirt Creek, just above where the creek runs into the Grand River.

He was raised here as was his father, and his father's father. Walking down the hill with measured steps one noticed his military attitude. And why not, he came from a long line of warriors. From before the coming of the white man they were called Akicita. Now they were called Veterans, and the family cemetery, called Pine and Little Eagle, included Veterans from the Army, Air Force and Marine Corps.

The man had come to see his father.

When things weren't going so well, or if a problem arose that needed someone more than his attention alone could resolve, he came home...and the old man knew it.

The old man didn't have to talk. He always seemed to know when his son would be coming, and in preparation he had built a campfire and had put two tree stumps where they would be sitting as they talked.

He knew that the evening would be chilly.

The man needed to be here, away from everything and everyone. He needed the solitude to reset his mind, slow down the pace, and get his priorities reorganized.

The man realized he never had to share his problems with his father. He just showed up and waited until his father was ready...and his father usually came out with a story that put the man's thoughts back into perspective.

The man offered the old man a beer in silence, then he lit a cigarette and offered one to the older man too. They drank their beer in silence, and after the third one the old man left to relieve himself. When he returned and reseated himself, the story began...

"One day the old woman from across the river came to see your grandmother..."

"She said that he had left again...that he had started to drink more often...sometimes he would go to town and be gone for days..."

"But this last time...he had brought something home with him..."

"He talks to 'it' all the time...as if he is actually having a conversation with another person...that's why I came here...to stay with you until its safe to return home again..."

"The old woman left a few days later...They had 3 boys and 3 girls but they were pretty much into their teens by that time, and a few of them had already left home to work and be on their own..."

"Then the old woman came again...and this time she was more frightened..."

"You could tell by her gait that she thought she was being followed...sometimes she would stop and look all around, as if trying to see who was following her..."

"Your grandmother was making wastukala by that time, but she started preparing her guest a plate... so by the time she arrived, she could finish having dinner with us...but by the time the old lady from across the river got here, she was beyond caring to eat..."

"She was all out of breath, and she was tired...as if she hadn't slept for a few days...but she couldn't wait to tell your grandmother what was happening now..."

"She said that whatever 'it' was, 'it' was with him all the time now...it was also now taking form..."

"She said that he would offer it some of whatever he was drinking...and for the first time last night, she could hear it set the bottle down..."

" And for the first time, also last night, she could see it in the dark...not clearly...but like a shadow...and it was smoking!"

"YES!"

"She could see the faint glow of the cigarette ash as it took a drag, and she could also smell the cigarette smoke!...and she somehow knew that it was a man..."

"The old woman stayed longer this visit and she helped your grandmother finish her wastukala. Then they started to can the wild fruit when she decided to go home..."

"Before she left she said that if he continued to carry on like that, she was going to move into town and he could stay with his friend."

The young man stood up and started up the hill to get more cigarettes and beer from his truck. But he stopped to watch the setting sun and the breathtaking view he missed so much, living in the city. The dog accompanied him up the hill to his truck and marked his territory on the truck tires.

When he returned, the story continued...

"We heard the old woman from across the river moved to town that same day..."

"We heard she stayed with one of their girls who was renting a big house in town..."

"Then we heard the old man from across the river stayed for awhile by himself too, but he eventually followed her into town and he also stayed at his daughter's place..."

"By this time he was selling his beef left and right...and he eventually bought the big house his daughter was renting..."

"One day your grandmother saw the old woman in town and they had a talk..."

"She said that whatever it was that was living with him out in the country had also followed him into town...and it's living with us right now!"

"But that isn't all!"

"Now it is starting to move the furniture...and when it walks you can hear it's footsteps on the hardwood flooring..."

"But now, he argues with it, as if it's a real person, and he's starting to tell it to leave him alone now...he can't sleep at night because it wants to talk to him all the time now, and now...I am really frightened!"

"Well, one day the oldest son went to the old man's house and they started drinking together...and the next day, when the old man wakes up...he says to her, " its gone..."

"He looked for it all over the house...but it was gone."

"So she thinks that maybe...now he could have some peace..."

"One day the oldest son went to the old man's house again and told him that something was living with him and his family..."

"He said it was like having another person living with them in their house...only you couldn't see this other person...but you could tell when it was around because you could smell it..."

"He said it smelled like a drunken person who hadn't taken a bath for some time..."

"Life went on as usual for the old man from across the river and his wife and daughters, but then he started to drink quite heavily again, only this time he was drinking more with his older kids on weekends and when they came home for the holidays."

"Then one day the police were called to the oldest son's house..."

"It seems, someone had beaten him up with a baseball bat...did a real good job of it too!"

"Some blame the wife..."

"They say she took a lover...and that the oldest son had caught them in bed together... and that a fight had occurred...and that the lover had killed the oldest son in a fight over the woman..."

"Then some say that the woman was beaten up by the oldest son because he had caught her with someone else in bed...and that she had killed him after he had fallen asleep after a night of drinking and fighting..."

"After the funeral, there was a drunken party, and everyone cried over their fallen brother..."

"After a couple of days everyone went back to their homes...in different parts of the country."

"But someone had noticed the old man at the drunken party...that he was acting real strange..."

"They say that he was talking to someone again... and this time he was cussing and telling "it" to leave him and his family alone..."

"After the family had disbursed, the old man was at peace again, but that wasn't going to last..."

"It wasn't long when they found the body of the second son lying on the railroad tracks with his head cut off..."

"Again there was a drunken party after the funeral...and again the old man was crying and cussing and telling "it" to leave his family alone..."

"The old lady from across the river never came to visit your grandmother anymore, but there was sure a lot of talk in town about the goings on at the house where they lived..."

"It seems they all started to drink more heavily and more often now...because whatever "it" was...was not around anymore...or so they thought."

"The next one to go was the second oldest daughter..."

"It seems there was a big party in town at a different house, and the second oldest girl attended...they say that she was the only girl there...anyway, sometime during the party someone had called her outside and had cut her throat from ear to ear..."

"They say that no one missed her, but one of the guys happened to find her as he was leaving to get some more alcohol..."

"This time the oldest girl didn't come back to bury her sister...and the youngest sister was in college and she couldn't afford to come home either, so it was up to the mom and dad, and the youngest brother to bury the middle sister..."

"Again...there was a big party and the old man was cussing and crying and pleading with "it" to leave his family alone...but everyone thought it was the strain of losing three of his kids in such a short period of time...so no one paid much attention."

"You'd think they would have learned by now, but they just kept right on drinking and drinking...every night...all night, every day...all day."

"It was during the 4th of July that anyone last saw the youngest son alive..."

"He was at the rodeo and carnival in town with some of his friends..."

"They say he had borrowed some clothes from one of his friends since the celebration was so long and he hadn't taken along an extra change of clothing with him..."

"They found him just below that rocky butte above the old place..."

"At first they couldn't recognize him because of the way he looked...they say he was bloated so badly that his clothing could have burst right off his body..."

"They also thought he was someone else...because of the clothing he was wearing...but I guess the worst part is, they say that his skin was so black from the sun that he must have been out there for quite some time before he was found...no one knows how long he was laying out there like that."

"After the funeral the old woman from across the river was the next one to go."

"Some say she had a heart attack, then some say that she was frightened to death, then some say that whatever "it" was, had come back and took her..."

"The old man from across the river never had another drink, but that didn't make no difference...because he left too...but some say he never did leave..."

"Some say he turned into that thing he called up from the other side..."

"Some say that all the killings and suicides that have been happening on the reservation have been done by him...or that thing he called up..."

"Now, no one knows how to get rid of it.."

"Anyway, the oldest daughter and the youngest daughter never did come home, instead, they had the old house torn down and the place leveled..."

And with that...the story was ended...

The man picked up all the empty beer cans and put them back into the bag in back of the pickup...then he returned to the campfire with his sleeping bag.

...the old dog lay by the fire... staring into the coals...staring...

Hau!

A WARRIORS PRAYER

From the Author

When I was 19 years old I enlisted in the Marine Corps and I was looking forward to going to Viet Nam and experiencing "Combat".

Before leaving for Viet Nam I was on leave and my Grandmother took me aside and asked me what was in my heart, what was the reason I was looking forward to going to combat? She explained that during a War, many bad things happen, and although many young men do not want to participate, they too are sometimes drawn into doing some bad things to those they have beaten.

When she was done explaining what the soldiers had done to our people, she told me to say this prayer with her...after we said the prayer together she said that if I said this prayer every morning and every evening I would return home unharmed.

She said the prayer is "similar" to those the old Warriors said in their day to day lives, but that this would be my prayer. In repeating the words daily I would remember what I was taught, and how I would conduct myself, and how I would have compassion on those less fortunate than I.

I know that today no one teaches their children such things, and for that reason I am sharing this prayer, if only to give you an insight of what relationship our People had with the Great Spirit.

First we must acknowledge the Great Spirit, then we must humble ourselves before him, and we must also acknowledge him for all the good things he has allowed us to have, including our health and life. Then when we ask him for something, it must be for the People, we do not ask for anything for ouselves, but always for the People.

A Warriors place in Lakota Society was only to "Protect and to Serve", in every sense of the word...and to keep the "Law". The "Law" was to provide for the widow, the orphan, and the elderly.....and those less fortunate. And yet to be known as a Warrior was to have the very highest esteem and honor one could bestow on another.

As you can see, today's non-native cultures have adopted these saying and have put them on police cars, and in the welfare programs, even up to the Federal Government level.

i.e. The Veterans Administration was established by President Abraham Lincoln for "The Widow, the Orphan and to care for him who shall have born the battle"...after the Battle of Gettysburg.

And now, A Warriors Prayer...

Hau!

A WARRIORS PRAYER

A poem
by
Eya Mani

Oh Great Spirit most Powerful,
humbly I come before you today,
I have come to ask of you one favor, if you would grant it,
I ask you for my adversary today,

Oh Great Spirit,
I ask that you would make him a good man, and a just man,
I ask that he be a man the people have looked up to and respected,
I ask that you would also make him a man of great strength and courage,

Oh Great Spirit,
you have given me a good life and good health,
and I thank you for that,
and I thank you for all that you have allowed me to have,
a place among the people, and a place among the warriors,

Oh Great Spirit,
Creator of Heaven and Earth,
I humbly come before you to ask of you this small favor,
so if I should fall, I will not be ashamed,
and I will have no excuse, and I will not have reason to be afraid
when I stand before you again,
Thank You, Oh Great Spirit

Hau!
(Thank you Grandma)

WATEHICA

From the Author

This week, another of our respected elders has gone on to make the journey alone, and this brings to mind the rest of our relatives and friends who have also left us and gone on alone.

What have they left us? What tracks have they left so we, or others may follow?

This also brings another questions forward...what am I leaving for my children? Will they be able to see my footprints? Have they listened while I tried to teach them what I was taught?

Probably the most troubling question I have is...what kind of life will they have after I also take my leave of them and go on alone?

My grandfather was a veteran of the USArmy, and the USAir Force, and he was a cook during WWII and Korea...

After his discharge, he was promised a 'bonus' from the USGovernment, for his outstanding service to his country...and in this next story, we find him waiting...and waiting...and waiting. Finally to make ends meet, he finally has to sell off his most prized possessions, his team of Belgian horses.

This story is a glimpse of the final hours of that event, and of what my uncle shared with me...leaving his tracks forever indelible in my mind...as did my grandfather, with his quiet strength...

I wish I could have such character...but now, my next offering...

WATEHICA...That Which You Hold Dear...

Hau!
(for uncle Elmer)

WATEHICA
(that which you hold dear, not easily parted with or replaced)

A Short Story
by
Eya Mani

The little boy had been sitting on his grandfather's lap most of the morning.

He knew that his grandfather felt bad about something but he didn't understand because he was so young, perhaps 4 or 5 years old.

He had his head on his grandfather's chest and he could hear his heartbeat and hear him breathing…occasionally his grandfather would take a deep breath and sigh.

Everyone else was still asleep.

He and his grandfather always got up early, and this morning he helped get the fire started in the old wood cook stove that his grandmother loved so much…it was her pride and joy.

When he and his grandfather went after a load of wood, his grandfather would gather only those smaller dry branches of cottonwood and tell the young boy, "This is the best wood for making bread, grandma sure likes to use this kind of wood when she cooks…"

So they had two piles of wood, one pile had larger branches, and the other, the kind grandma liked to cook with.

The boy turned to his grandfather and straightened his shirt collar, then he hugged him and got off his lap and went outside.

The village was still dark but the dawn was breaking and he could see the smoke slowly rising from the other log houses in the village. The birds had been up singing for a while now and the dogs started to bark and wake up the rest of the village.

This was the best part of the day…smoke smells, birds singing, dogs barking, and the smell of coffee brewing and food cooking.

There was activity in the corrals below the house, and someone was whistling a tune, so he strained his eyes to see what was going on down there.

It was his uncle, he had already hitched up the team of Belgian horses to the wagon and he had also loaded an empty 50 gallon drum onto the wagon, along with a pitchfork and a manure fork. Then while the boy watched, he drove the wagon up to the house and got *down, and they both went inside.*

This uncle was never quiet.

He slammed the door as he came inside and stepped heavily on the wooden floor, making sure he woke those still sleeping. He greeted the old ones then asked if the coffee was ready and if there was anything ready to eat.

Everyone spoke the language and the boy listened intently, not wanting to miss anything discussed. Maybe he would find out why his grandfather's heart was so heavy. When there was a break in the discussion, he asked his uncle what he was going to do today with the pitchforks and the barrel in the wagon.

"Fish Friday" his uncle said, then "Oooooohhhhhaaayyyyy!!!, then he laughed loudly and said, "When the meat runs out, then we have fish, there's always something for us if we get up early and go after it."

"If you want to catch fish in a hurry, get ready, I'll show you how to catch the biggest ones without a line and hook, and without getting wet...we won't be long."

"Shall I wake the others then?"

"No, let them sleep...maybe they need their rest, maybe someday they'll be able to buy their fish instead of catching it, but come, let's go before the sun comes up."

As they bounced along the wagon road leading to the river he felt bad because his grandfather was quiet that morning. They had read the Bible with grandma and said prayers but that still didn't seem to make him feel any better. Usually he felt better after his prayers were said, but not this morning...

As they neared the river crossing, his uncle turned the team to the deepest part of the river and drove the wagon into the water, then stopped when the water was up to the wagon box.

All the while his uncle was whistling and humming and the boy liked that.

He remembered some of the tunes from the old radio his grandmother had...grandpa had to hookup the old dry cell battery and wire antennae for reception. Then they would listen to the "World Today" and Paul Harvey.

Then grandpa would take the radio apart again and put it away...

Sometimes they would listen to KOLY, but only when one of his uncles was playing guitar and singing gospel hymns on Sundays. Then, even the neighbors came to listen and sometimes sing along...

His uncle rolled a smoke and sat quietly until he finished his smoke...

The boy knew enough not to talk when they were fishing, or to move around either, but his uncle didn't seem to follow the rules...and he wondered how they were going to catch any fish if his uncle wasn't quiet?

His uncle picked up the pitchfork and shouted, "Here they come!"...the boy hadn't noticed before but the fishes where already swimming around the wagon and team.

His uncle had been waiting for the really big catfish to swim by...now they were coming and he was ready.

With their heads swinging from side to side, as if parading and showing off, the huge catfish came...seeming to offer themselves to the man with the pitchfork. The boy had to take a deep breath...he had never seen catfish this big! He had only caught the "pan-size" on his homemade fishing pole.

"This one is for Mrs. Grey Eagle...this one is for Old Frank...this one is for Mrs. Bear Rib...this one is for my sister." He went on naming people who were going to have fish that day...and one after another the fish came and he speared them with the pitchfork and tossed them into the barrel.

After the sun topped the east hill the fish all went under water, as if on cue.

When the fish stopped coming, his uncle took a bucket from under the seat and filled the barrel with river water, then he rolled another smoke and sat quietly watching the smoke rise in the calm cool air.

"That's how you catch the big one's..." his uncle shouted as he turned the team around in the water. And he laughed his belly laugh and he started whistling again...

"But you have to get up early enough to get ready, and make sure you get enough for everyone."

The boy was standing...holding onto the barrel...watching the catfish move around, and he ventured a question,

"Uncle, why is grandpa thinking so hard...?"

"Sometimes we have to do things we don't want to do. Grandpa has to make a decision today, but he knows best. I wanted to show you this before it was too late...now whatever will happen...will happen."

The boy and his uncle made the rounds delivering the early morning prize and they came back to the house just before the noon meal.

There was a big truck waiting at the corral and he knew why grandpa was so sad...

Hau!

WHERE DID YOU GET YOUR DUCT TAPE TRAINING?

From the Author

We were visiting in the cool of the evening when the subject of duct tape came up.

It seems silly but there are so many uses we Lakota have for it, it seems to have taken the place of baling wire and barbed wire for quick auto repairs.

Our friend Leslie made a comment that her son got his duct tape training from such and such a person and place and it seemed logical that we should expound on its many and varied uses.

I once saw my brother cut a commodity milk can down the middle, put it around his exhaust pipe and tape it up. Just like new!!! and he didn't get it Midasized either!!!

So with tongue in cheek we take a quick look at what duct tape has become, from Astronauts to Lakota on the Rez, we sing the praises of duct tape.

And now my next offering..."WHERE DID YOU GET YOUR DUCT TAPE TRAINING?"

Hau!

"WHERE DID YOU GET YOUR DUCT TAPE TRAINING...?"

A Short Story
by
Eya Mani

Throughout the years I've come to appreciate duct tape, and as one guy I worked with once said, "You have to respect everything you work with", so in that regard I guess you can say I respect duct tape.

Of course in order to fully appreciate Duct tape and its many uses, one has to see the tape in action, and so my introduction and training began...

One day in 1974 I was cruising South along 1806 Highway by the Oak Creek bridge, just below the St. Elizabeth's Mission when I had a vision...standing west of the bridge along the water was three Lakota women washing Taniga.

I slammed on the brakes and pulled off the road in a cloud of dust, (and I will cherish this moment forever) I could hear the group 'ABBA' singing "Gimme Gimme Gimme a Man after Midnight" blaring on the radio. (Sigh)

The effect was sheer magic...

This was probably the second time that I would meet my future wife and "in-laws" doing what Lakota do best...clean Taniga...

Of course not wanting to pass up a chance for 'Gutmeat and Turnips...', I hopped out of my road machine and helped them clean the remaining Taniga.

While working with the ladies and making small talk I noticed something strange...everything was taped up.

The knife handles were bound in duct tape, the old washtub that held the Taniga was taped up, the old pickup truck window was taped up, and I think but am not sure, but I remember pumping up one of the truck tires and I'm sure that it was wrapped in duct tape too!

Not wishing to appear the 'fool' I said nothing, but on closer inspection I noticed that this thing called duct tape seemed to take on a magical mystical appearance. Even the family dog had on a duct tape bandage around his leg!!!

Later driving down McLaughlin's main street I thought I'd better keep an eye out for more uses of what I am now sure is one of Wakan Tanka's gifts to the Lakota...

One of my cousins was parked along the street with the car hood up so I stopped to see if I could offer assistance. But he had everything in control, when he pulled out his roll of duct tape and started wrapping up his radiator hose, I breathed a sigh of relief! I knew he would get home safely with his family. Then I noticed that all the wire splices on his battery cable, starter wiring, and alternator, were also repaired with duct tape. Even some of his vacuum hoses were patched with duct tape.

Then one of my uncle's walked up and asked what the trouble was? My cousin had dropped his roll of duct tape, and as I bent to retrieve it, low and behold!!!, my uncle had his boots wrapped in duct tape...!!! "Wow" I thought..."Just think of the savings!!!"

One of my cousins used to ride on the circuit...before he got into the chutes he would tape up above and below his knees with duct tape over his Wranglers...I think it acted as a knee brace more or less, so this magical tape was also very important in the area of Health Care and Accident Prevention too...(I don't mean that kind of accident either!!)

Of course, being a musician in my brothers band, we had other uses for duct tape. For instance, Roger used it to hold his Ghost pedal together so he could keep the beat, but he also used it to keep his cymbals on their stands and hold his broken drum sticks together, and when the music was flowing and he didn't want to quit, he would patch his drum heads with this most resilient of substances...then sometimes it could be used ornamentally too, and its household uses are many and varied.

For instance you could patch that hole in the wall where your cousin's head went thru...all you have to do is cut a square cardboard and tape the edges and then you can paint over this patch!!! No one would ever know unless you decide to stick your cousin thru the wall again...

In 25 years of marriage the education I've received from the Mrs. is far reaching and on going, and now it educational benefits are generational...our kids each carry their own roll...

We've sealed our windows and doors with it, but lately we use it more to hold the TV remote together, so the batteries will stay inside...other wise you gotta get up and change the channels by hand.

This is bad for us larger more 'fluffy' folks, cause once you get up to change the channels...what the heck huh?, you might as well go to the fridge and make another sandwich...

In the right hands duct tape has saved lives.

Just think what peril the Astronauts would have been in if they had only 'cotton balls and tampons' up in space? But with duct tape they were able to make a filter for cleaner air and thus return safely to Earth.

Of course we Lakota are not so sinister as some other folks of questionable heredity who also use duct tape...which seems to be a favorite of hostage takers, bank robbers, mass murderers and that sort of riff raff...

No Sirree Boy...we Lakota are more genteel when it comes to the use of duct tape.

I can't say if its true or not...but the word behind the chutes is, that one cowboy didn't want to wear a 'cup' for fear it would do more harm to his future generations, so he opted for a roll of duct tape.

Hats off to this brave lad for breaking new ground!!! What other and more innovative uses will we think of next?

Hau!
(for Leslie)

"YOU KNOW WHO YOU ARE AND YOU KNOW WHAT YOU DID!"

From the Author

   Humor plays a very important part of Lakota Culture.

   Whenever you see a group of men or women doing something together, you can be sure that they are also telling funny stories and laughing.

   Sometimes to take the edge off, little stories are made up and told to see if anyone is paying any attention to what is being said or what is going on...

   Because of the brevity of these very short stories I will tell them and hope that the humor comes through as intended...

   As with all Lakota stories...I tell these stories with tongue-in-cheek and you must pay particular attention...sometimes its best to clear your mind of everything, take off your shoes and relax...

   And now my next offering..."YOU KNOW WHO YOU ARE AND YOU KNOW WHAT YOU DID..."

Hau!
(for Georgie...)

"YOU KNOW WHO YOU ARE AND YOU KNOW WHAT YOU DID..."

A
Short Story
by
Eya Mani

The young men had been sitting around on the flatbed box of the old pickup truck, which was littered with boxes of spare and replacement parts, oil cans and grease guns.

Owen was reading a comic book and Joe was sitting in the passenger side of the cab of the old truck with his legs dangling out the open door, he had his head back and his eyes closed...but everyone was sweating freely in the hot July weather.

The boys had been putting up hay for their grandfather, but they'd had a flat tire on the old truck on their way back home for lunch. Now, because of the heat and their hunger, none of them volunteered to change the tire or help another to change the tire. Rather, they were moving quietly into the small amount of shade the truck offered...perhaps hoping the heat would not know they were there and would ignore them??

The men were all cousins and they usually interacted well together, but the heat was just too much for them, so they just sat quietly wiping their sweat, waiting for some one to make the first move...

Finally George, who was lying underneath the pickup box on the ground said...
"Hey, you guys ever see two snakes fight?"
... no answer...
...not even a stir...
... "I did!"...
..." once"...
... still no answer...but he continued anyway...

"It was over by the White Coat Corner...I was hunting just after the rain."

"I was walking west across the flat when I came on this 'hardpan' and I saw this bull snake crawling toward the 'hardpan'..."

"Then I saw this rattlesnake coming from this other way..."

"At first, I thought they would pass each other and go their own way, but they both stopped to check each other out."

"The bull snake was the first to make a move...he came right up to the rattlesnake like he was going to smell him...and the rattlesnake just sorta backed off."

"Then the two snakes just came together at the same time...but the rattlesnake didn't do nothing."

"I thought he would start biting...because that's what they do...but he didn't."

"Instead the bull snake just wrapped himself around the rattlesnake and started tightening...like those constrictor snakes do!...just tighten up and relax...and tighten up and relax."

"All this time the rattlesnake didn't do nothing except suffer...you could see he was suffering...but he must have been getting mad now cause he would show his teeth once in awhile...but still he didn't bite neither!"

George waited a few minutes...but no one moved or made a sound...so he continued...

"I was gonna shoot them both...but I was curious to see which one would win, so I just kept on watching."

"All of a sudden, the bull snake must have thought he had the rattlesnake where he wanted him because he started to swallow him up...only he started at the tail...I always thought they swallowed the head first!"

George waited again before continuing...but still no one moved or made a sound.

"Anyway, the bull snake had about a foot of this rattlesnake swallowed up when the rattlesnake started to swallow up the bull snake too!...and he started swallowing from the tail too!!"

"Well, I wanted to watch this so I sat down and got comfortable and I rolled a smoke..."

"Next, the bull snake waited until the rattlesnake caught up with him...now they were both swallowed up about halfway, and they were laying there on the ground like a circle..."

"They kept swallowing and swallowing each other...and the circle just kept getting smaller and smaller...and pretty soon they were almost done!"

Owens had put his comic book down and the others had gotten a little closer to hear this most amazing tale of nature...

But George just closed his eyes and went to sleep...the rest of the guys just looked at each other until one of them asked George what happened next?

George said "HUH? Oh!...I didn't think you guys were listening...because no one said anything."

"Anyway, I don't know what happened either, because they both got done at the same time, I don't know which one won."

Joe asked, "What do you mean you don't know which one won? I thought you were watching them all this time?"

George said "I was...only when they got done they were gone...just disappeared...they swallowed each other up! You know that when you swallow something its gone?...just like that!"

Hau!

ZEZECA

From the Author

Zezeca (Snake) was written in Spearfish, SD in February of 2000.

It is intended merely as a learning tool, and to make people think of all the outside influences that fashion and shape our lives, whether real or imagined...

In our story overwhelming poverty, unemployment, and hunger forced our main character to act rashly, but forgiveably so.

If our main character would have taken the other "option" he had been thinking about, the story would have ended and we would be left without anything to think about. And so is Lakota storytelling. We must leave the listeners something which they can take with them from our storytelling circle.

As I make my new home here, in a new land, a new town, and in a new millenium, with many new friends to also meet and make, I hope that the Spirit that brought me here will allow me to create and write in the manner the 'old ones' would approve of. Our stories must be told and that without prejudice or consequence.

As I can remember and create these stories, I give thanks to Wakan Tanka daily for his blessings that he has allowed me to share. I pray that I would always remain worthy of these gifts...

And now, my offering "ZEZECA"...

Hau!
(for my cousin, Jerry)

ZEZECA

A Short Story
by
Eya Mani

The man had been standing on the south rim of the hill, overlooking the Hump Creek, which lay below to the north.

It had taken him many hours to reach this point in his hunt for food, and now he stood looking down at the weapons that lay on the ground at his feet.

He had counted and recounted the ammunition he carried for each of the three weapons he had brought with him...now he took the K-bar from its scabbard, and he checked the blade. Earlier that morning, he had spent hours honing it to a razors edge...

This was the last place he was going to cover in his hunt for wild game, and he was now out about 15 miles from his home in Rock Creek.

He rolled a smoke, sat down and lit it.

Then he let his eyes survey his intended avenue of approach. He knew full well, that there would be no food on the table for his family that night...as he put out his cigarette, he hung his head and wept silently...but no tears came.

He knew what he had to do...the choices were not many...so he picked up the 30.06 he had brought for big game, and threw a round into the chamber, and wiped his tears.

He suddenly noticed, that since his arrival to this vantage place unseen...and even as he made his way here, he had not seen or heard any birds or insects...this was very strange.

Back home in Rock Creek, a young mother and three hungry children awaited the return of their father who they hoped would be successful this time, but also knowing that there was no wild game in that part of the country.

The young woman's husband was a fine young man, recently discharged from the Marines...he had pride and integrity and he was proud of his family. But times were bad and the rivers and creeks had long since dried up. And the wild game either simply left the country or died of starvation or thirst as so many domestic animals had perished.

The time was the mid-1950's...

During the young hunter's absence, events had occurred that brought joy to his wife and family back home.

It seems a young female cow had been trying to drink water from a culvert on the road to their grandmother's home, and it had gotten its head caught in the culvert and had broken its neck, trying to escape.

The rancher who owned the heifer, had bled the animal and had brought it to her grandmother's home for butchering.

The young hunter rolled another smoke and sat thinking...weighing the outcome of his decision. He knew he would hurt his family either way, but his pride and honor would not let him change his mind.

He had not taken any food at home for two days now. Instead, he let his children eat his share, and instead of making him feel better about himself, he was still feeling hopeless.

All the while, his young wife tried to be playful and bring up happier times that they'd shared...he knew she was going to miss him terribly.

He now felt the effects of his fast, and the hot July weather did not help any...

On his trek out here his vision was becoming blurred and his sweat had stopped, and he was starting to get a headache...

He now had a very great thirst, but he would look for water later...perhaps in one of the many creeks below he would find enough water to replace that which he lost...perhaps.

Just as he was getting to his feet, he saw movement on one of the many trails below, so he sat back and hunkered down...then, rising just enough to peer over the hilltop through the grass.

He wiped his eyes so he could make sure of what he had seen...and his mind raced!

Whatever it was, it was coming up the draw directly toward him...but at a snails pace.

It seemed to be following the cow path along the bottom of the draw he had intended to cover first...licking his lips, he rose slowly again and peered through the grass...and his mind raced on...wait...wait.

He had heard all the old stories of such things...but he never really believed in them, ...well...maybe only as entertainment, or so he had thought.

Now he wasn't so sure...

The old ones tell tales of large animals and beasts that come out during bad times such as these...and the absence of the game is attributed to their presence.

Whether the wild game had fled the country for fear of them, or whether they had indeed been devoured by these creatures...is unknown.

But here was one now...and he was going to meet it face to face...and if he survived, he would know first hand.

Again he leaned forward and kneeling, he peered through the grass. This time he watched it a bit longer, before he settled back down to think about this...

The creature was unlike any he had ever seen, heard, or read about...

This creature was as tall as a large dog, and through the shimmering heat, he thought that it was transparent...he seemed able to see through portions of it.

Its tongue was continually flicking in and out of its mouth...testing the breezes that floated down the creek.

It had obviously "smelled" something and it was definitely headed his way...and the thought of him being its next meal frightened him, for he surely couldn't kill it...not with the weapons he had at hand...it was too large!

On its journey up the hill toward him, the beast dropped out of sight, so he crawled towards the edge of the hilltop to get a better look.

Now he was sure...this creature had detected his presence and it was coming for him...

When he realized he was the intended next meal, he quickly rose to his feet and gathered the weapons, loading each to capacity, he made sure his K-bar was ready...then he looked down the steep hill at his approaching foe.

Knowing the speed normal size snakes could attain, he knew he had little time, but he would make a stand...he knew this monster snake would run him down in no time flat... so he very cautiously approached the edge of the hilltop.

From this vantage point, he would have a clear view and field of fire toward his approaching enemy.

As the huge snake came charging up the hill, he could now see its muscles moving under its skin, bringing the monster closer at an alarming rate!

He lay the larger caliber weapons down, and with precision shots, he emptied the 17 rounds from the .22 rifle into the creature's head, thinking "this should at least slow the damn thing down."

The huge snake hesitated for just a second, then, with increased speed, it restarted its charge up the hill.

He could not tell if he had done any damage, but he slung the .22, then he picked up the 30.06 next and took careful aim...adrenaline was flowing and his vision had cleared, and he knew exactly what he must do if he were to survive...

He again emptied his weapon into the head of the advancing creature, making sure his shots were centered between the creature's eyes. But he had no way of knowing if his shots were doing any damage...this creature didn't bleed!

If he was to live, then he must do something...but he must do it now.

He picked up the 12 gauge shotgun and threw a round into the chamber.

The shotgun held only 5 rounds, but he knew that would probably give him enough time to get past this creature, buy him some time, but either way, it was now or never...

With his renewed strength, the keenness of his vision and the clarity of his thought returned... and he knew he didn't want to die this way.

Never to be found, seen or heard from again...

He would just be another "missing person" that everyone would talk about, but eventually, someone would find his weapons and expended shell casings and everyone would make up stories of what had happened to him... and he didn't want to die this way.

As he reslung his two rifles over his shoulder, he undid the snap holding his K-bar in place...now he was ready.

Taking a deep breath, he let out an extended shout, and charged headlong down the hill, directly toward the advancing beast...

He continued shouting as he ran, but he waited until he was almost on top of the still approaching monster, that he fired his first shot...laying open a flap of skin...but still he could see no blood...

The monster stopped this time, but whether from confusion or from the punishment he was meting out, he did not know or care.

He just jacked another round into the chamber and fired into the animals head, peeling back the skin exposing bone...but still no blood.

Still shouting, he charged right past the monster, firing as he ran, emptying his shotgun into the body of the creature as he flew by...each shot opening up the creatures skin... exposing torn and shredded muscles...but this time he drew blood.

He could see that his shots had indeed hurt this creature...good!

"I just might get out of this alive," he thought as he raced on down the hill...

Three days later he came to...and he was at home, sitting in a chair at his own table.

His wife had prepared a wonderful meal for him and she was trying to coax him into eating.

They say that he had been brought home by one of the neighbors who happened to be coming home from town that evening...they say they had found him running on the road, and when they stopped to ask him where he was going, he just got in without a word.

But they said he had no rifles or ammunition...and the scabbard for his K-bar was empty as well...

The young man got up from the table without a word and he walked to the river and jumped in with all his clothes on, and he just sat there. After a couple of hours of sitting in the big mud puddle that was the river, he returned home, took a bath and changed his clothes.

And finally he did eat...all the while, never saying a word to anyone about what had happened to him.

When the young man finally broke his silence...four days had passed since his return.

It was the evening of the fourth day, when the men were gathered around the shade visiting and telling stories, that the young man came to the circle.

He told what had happened to him...he spoke of his fear...and what he had felt, and when he was finished he got up and went home and went to bed.

The men sitting around the shade didn't have any more stories to tell...they just rolled smokes and thought about it...and they knew what they had to do.

The young man with the beautiful young wife, arose early the next day, put on his best clothing, kissed his wife who was still asleep, and walked out of the village.

About the same time that same morning, the men saddled their best horses and left before daybreak...they were all armed and three hours later they were overlooking the breaks where the young man had first seen this monster snake.

"Geez, that's too bad...ennit?" the old cowboy said after a very long silence...then,

"You know...I didn't think that they would ever come out this far...?"

...then after another long silence...

"They only come out around the Missouri...but it's usually at times like these...and you just never know..."

The riders had been letting the horses catch their breath after the exertion of a long steady gait on their way out here...now they just sat on their horses and rolled smokes, while surveying the carnage below... never saying a word, only the old cowboy had spoken.

Below them...in the trail along the draw leading up the hill, lay eight dead pigs.

Indeed a slaughter had occurred here...but the young man would never know...he would never return to the village, neither would his wife and children ever hear from him or see him again...

Hau!

A LESSON IN HUMILITY…

From the Author

It's been a few years since our journey to this village in the story to partake of their annual pow wow.

Every year, we make plans for including it on our "want to go do that list…" only it never seems to work out. Again this year its on my list of places to go, but only time can tell if that will be possible…

As pow wow time rolls around again, I have to sit and remember all those who I've met and befriended along the way…and it just makes me smile…

I imagine one of the two mechanics in this next story, will read my next offering some day, and have a good laugh remembering…and I hope they now have a car they won't have to "time" while its in motion.

This is a tribute to all "shade tree mechanics" who just have to get to the very next pow wow, no matter what…and now, my next offering… "A Lesson In Humility…"

Hau!

A LESSON IN HUMILITY...

A Short Story
by
Eya Mani

We had arrived the night before around midnight, and while my friend and I put up the tipi, my wife and our friends unpacked.

We had to use the headlights from the pickup truck, and in no time we had the tipi up and tied down, and our camping stuff safe inside...just in time too, because the storm was rolling in.

This was my first pow wow in Red Scaffold...a fairly small community on the Cheyenne River Reservation. But my wife's family was from these parts, and although the attendance was not that great, it proved to be one of the very best pow wow's that I had attended up to that time.

After we had put up our tipi, we decided to turn in for the night. The pow wow had just broken up from the first night of celebration, we call camping night, and as we lay in our tipi, all safe and warm, the storm hit...the wind first...then the driving rain.

We could see car lights flashing around on our tipi, and people were shouting and running around. Women were screaming, kids were crying, and dogs were barking...

Eventually this all stopped, as everyone settled in for the night again. But early the next morning, as my friend and I were taking a morning walk along the creek, we could see the damage that the storm had done during the night.

It was the first day of pow wow, and already only two shelters were standing. Ours, and another family's who had also set up a tipi. Everyone else had brought store bought camp tents and other forms of shelter. And these had all blown down during the night...it looked like everyone else had slept in their vehicles, except us and that other family.

As my friend and I stood on the hill overlooking the scattered homes in the community, our attention was drawn to a particular house.

Two men were working on an older Chevy out in the yard, but they seemed to be having trouble getting the timing right. When they would apply the gas, the car would backfire and the engine would stop...then someone would cuss. They would take time and make their adjustments, and try it again...and it would backfire again, and the engine would stop...then we'd hear them cuss again.

"Vacuum hose..." my friend had said chuckling, "They won't get the timing right because the vacuum hose is broke or loose..."

After we had breakfast, my wife said she wanted to visit her brother who lived in the community...and introduce her friends to her family.

As we prepared to leave camp, we could hear the occasional backfire, which seemed to be getting louder and more frequent.

"Geez those guys..." my friend said, "Maybe we should go and help them out..."

The visit was short and pleasant, and we learned that the veterans needed a few more butchers to help prepare for the veterans feed. It is the custom for whoever puts on the feed...to kill, prepare and serve the people...so we had our work cut out for us.

On our way back to the pow wow grounds, we stopped at the store and bought bread, cigarettes and pop.

Just as we were leaving the parking lot, the car the two men had been working on earlier, flew past.

The hood was open and someone was laying outside on the fender with his head under the hood. When they would hit a pot hole, the man's legs would bounce and the hood would close on him, and we could hear him shout and swear, then the car would backfire again...

They went over the hill and out of sight...but we could still hear the occasional backfire fading in the distance...and we could imagine the man bounce and the hood close on him again...

I had to stop the truck because we were laughing so hard...we even got out of the truck and walked around a bit.

After we regained our composure and we caught our breath, my friend said, "Man, talk about dedication to your craft...I want those guys to work on my car...I know they'll get the job done, no matter what...I hope that guy under the hood makes it alright..."

Then we burst out into uncontrollable laughter again, so my wife said, "Quit now, you were like that when I met you...you're lucky I married you..." she teased. Then she went on, "I had to straighten you out...otherwise you and Pat would be doing that back at home...embarrassing me and the family...! "

This teasing only made us laugh harder...and we had to stop the truck again...

After we had finally gotten back to camp, I dug out our skinning knives and we went to help the veterans butcher.

As we worked with the other veterans, once in a while my friend and I would burst out laughing, thinking about those two mechanics...

One of the other veterans asked what we were laughing about...so I mentioned the two young men working on the car that morning, and I related what we had witnessed.

"Oh...those two...they always do things the hard way!"...he replied.

Hau!

THE BACK OF THE WOMAN'S FACE...

From the Author

In August of 1999 I realized I had been in a very dangerous depression...

Although I was aware that I had not written anything for a few months...nor had I made any of my arts and crafts, August was the most dangerous time of my life...

I had packed my bags, my sewing machines and what I thought I'd need...and I was ready to leave my wife, my kids, my friends, and my home...and go to Montana to seek peace, work, and try to regain my creative frame of mind.

My faith in my God was at its weakest point ever...and I had stopped the morning ritual of reading my 24 hours a day, my Bible, and my Day by Day book...in the past these daily readings would set my frame of mind to accommodate the days activities, yet unforeseen.

Thinking back...I realized that I had started drinking again...although, only on weekends...nevertheless, drinking again...which was completely out of character for me.

Before leaving my wife of 24 years, we had a heart to heart talk, and I decided to return my life back to my God...I asked him to return the gifts that he had given me...the gifts of creating beautiful things...my arts, my crafts, my writings, and my music...and that night I had a dream of what I was to do...

As the poem came together...so did my spirit and my faith in my God...and now I thank you, the reader, for allowing me the time to share my gifts with you...

And now, I offer you...The Back of the Woman's face...

Hau!

For Sandra...
My wife...my lover...my friend
September...1999

THE BACK OF THE WOMAN'S FACE...

A Poem
By
Eya Mani

Do you hear...?
The sound of a spirit dying...?
Someone's ideas...someone's hopes...someone's dreams dying...?
It's the sound of a Nation...dying

Have you heard...?
They say it was a car crash...and her only child lay dying
We all knew him...a good child...a cherished son
Alcohol has taken him...and the spirit of a Nation lay dying

Who can hear...?
The sound of a guitar...idle in a corner...?
or the beat of the drum...huddled silent on the floor
he will not again raise his voice...and the spirit of our Nation lay dying

We have heard...
The women went to ask for help...because their children lay dying
We heard they turned their backs on them...because they wanted our lands and water
While the spirit of our Nation lay dying

Do you hear...?
The sound of her youngest son rising...the sound of a warrior rising...?
Do you also hear...the sound of a smile returning...?
It is the sound of our People returning...

CALL THEM...AMERICANS

From the Author

   This is my first work of the new century...my poem simply states what has happened in the last century, to my people, the Lakota...and also to those of us who still believe that there is "good" somewhere in our great country.

   Monica and Bill shook us to the core, some of the other things are the debate over Creationism vs. Darwinism, the killing of "Boo" Many Horses in Mobridge SD in 1999, the widening gap of the haves and the have nots, the imprisoning of a Lakota man in SD for taking a can of beenie-weenie out of a parked car...he got 15 years for theft.

   If a people were to be judged by their actions...as they so nobly preach...then I would hate to be called an American.

   Even the earth is in turmoil...on January 7, 2000 it was 44 degrees in Mobridge, SD.

   Yet...all is not lost...we have to move on, but we cannot forget what we have done, so we will not make those same mistakes that we seem to be repeating all the time...

   I wish you readers well...as lovers of the written word I know we are more discerning than the average bear, and we see things differently than the average person on the street...and we have to remember not to take ourselves so seriously in the coming years.

   HAPPY NEW YEAR...

Hau!

CALL THEM...AMERICANS

A Poem
By
Eya Mani

They say they came here for religious freedom...

yet...they will idolize Freud

They came here with a Bible in their hands...

yet...they embrace Darwin

They say they want justice...

yet...they will plea bargain

They want to police the world...

yet...they will oppress their own

They send my people to prison for stealing food...

yet...they've stolen my land, my gold, and now they want my water

They want to be called good...clean...honest...and just...

I will call them Americans...I am Lakota

Hau!

Printed in the United States
By Bookmasters